C000242077

Don't Look

Don't Look Back in Anger

Also by Richard Kurt

United We Stood
Despatches From Old Trafford
As The Reds Go Marching On
Cantona
The Red Army Years

Don't Look Back in Anger

Growing up with Oasis

Chris Hutton and Richard Kurt

SIMON & SCHUSTER
A VIACOM COMPANY

First published in Great Britain by Simon & Schuster Ltd, 1997
A Viacom Company

Copyright © 1997 by Richard Kurt

This book is copyright under the Berne Convention.
No reproduction without permission.
All rights reserved.

The right of Richard Kurt and Chris Hutton to be identified as
authors of this work has been asserted by them in accordance
with sections 77 and 78 of the Copyright, Designs and Patents
Act 1988

1 3 5 7 9 10 8 6 4 2

Simon & Schuster Ltd
West Garden Place
Kendal Street
London W2 2AQ

Simon & Schuster Australia
Sydney

A CIP catalogue record for this book is available
from the British Library

ISBN 0-684-81956-2

Typeset in Meridien 11.5/14pt by
Palimpsest Book Production Limited, Polmont, Stirlingshire
Printed and bound in Great Britain by
The Bath Press, Bath

To the memory of Ian Curtis

'*Modern Life is Rubbish* – the rubbish of the past. We all live on it: it dictates our thoughts. And because it's all built up over such a long time, there's no necessity for originality anymore. There are so many things to splice together in infinite permutations that there is absolutely no need to create anything new. I think that phrase is the most significant comment on popular culture since "Anarchy in the UK". That's why I want to graffiti it everywhere. I think it expresses everything.'

Damon Albarn to the *NME*, 1993

Contents

A Note on the Contributors

On Joy Division: **Bob Dickinson** moved to Manchester in 1977. He's worked for Granada, Channel Four, and BBC Radio's One through Four. Before that, he wrote for the *NME, Observer, Guardian, City Life, Manchester Evening News* and *Blues & Soul*. His book on the alternative press, *Imprinting The Sticks*, was published by Arena/Ashgate in August 1997.

On the Smiths: **Pat Gilbert** is assistant editor of *Record Collector* and has also contributed to *Mojo, The Times* and the *Guardian*. Born in 1966, his loves include Blur, the Beach Boys, the Clash and golf; he was once described by Paul Weller as 'the most miserable journalist he'd ever met.'

On 'Madchester': **Stefan Pierlejewski** is one of Manchester's dance cognoscenti and the creative force behind both Beyond's 'A Positive Life' and 'Proton 1'. A producer, remixer and writer, he snorted, smoked and shimmied his way through every high and low-light of Manchester's 80s dance culture.

On the Happy Mondays: **John Robb** is a musician, producer and journalist who lives in Hulme, Manchester. Having written about every major Manchester band in his time from the closest of vantage points, he now leads his own group, Gold Blade, and will shortly have his definitive book about the Stone Roses published.

On the Stone Roses: **Mick Middles** has contributed on music and pop culture to every Mancunian publication worth writing for over the past decade and is currently resident at the *Evening News*. The first author to produce a proper account of Oasis's story with *Round Their Way*, his most recent addition to a personal library of Manc rock lit. detailed the adventures of Shaun Ryder.

Preface

I had never intended to produce this book. Until recently, it was enough for me to know that just those who mattered to me around Manchester recognized the role I'd played in the story of Oasis. I didn't care that the rest of the city and country had no idea: I turned a deaf ear to the phone calls from the tabloid press, who begged me to tell my tale. But when some members of the band – and, in particular, their hangers-on – began to criticize me in books, or sought to marginalize me, I decided to have my account published, if only to defend my reputation. When we finished it, I also realized that this might fill a gap in the history of the group and allow its fans to piece together the full picture at last.

But I never wanted this story to be just about Oasis. When I formed the group, we all wanted to be a *Manchester* band first and foremost; similarly, I wanted this book to be about growing up in our city and the influences all of Oasis felt in the 1980s.

That is why Richard Kurt, our contributors and I have talked about United and City, Madchester and the great post-punk Manchester bands as well – for our city was a world-beater long before Oasis came along, and will continue to be so long after they've gone. *Don't Look Back In Anger* is about growing up with Oasis – but also about what helped make us who we are.

Chris Hutton: Manchester, England, 1997

Acknowledgements

Thanks to BJ, Mark and Steve Shenton, Paddy and Danny Brown, John Hodkinson, Tony French and Jimmy Gregory.

Special thanks to the two most important people in my life, Elizabeth and Jorja.

Respect to Ian Brown for being the coolest man on earth.

And thanks to everyone who supported The Rain: they know who they are.

Chris Hutton, June 1997

I am indebted to Dave Marsh, Bob Dickinson, Stefan Pierlejewski, John Robb, Pat Gilbert and Mick Middles for agreeing to contribute their expertise, and to Andy Spinoza for sterling advice.

Thanks to Bill Campbell, Graham Beech and Ian Marshall for past and present support and especially to Julian Alexander and his team at the L.A.W. agency.

Well played to Emma for her patience.

And top thanks to Chris Hutton for getting his story so well sorted and for choosing me to tell it.

Richard Kurt, June 1997

Introduction:

There is a Light that Never Goes Out

Joy Division by Bob Dickinson

Joy Division weren't a punk band. But they came into existence as a result of punk. We need to think about punk first, because punk won't go away. Joy Division are dead, and in many ways are associated with death. But punk won't give up the ghost.

Punk is comfortable as an old armchair these days. Viv Westwood OBE is everyone's favourite authority, not just on fashion and design but the whole business of being British, a modern-day, north-country Dame Edith Sitwell. In 1996, there was a well-attended and widely reported twentieth anniversary punk weekend in Blackpool. And the Pistols reformed and played a tour of Europe, sounding on the films I saw of them pretty indistinguishable from most summer festival rock bands. People like punk. An authentic, eccentric English product, the invention of the mid-seventies, it underpins modern pop in Britain – from the sound of younger bands like Three Colours

Red, Tiger, or Symposium, to established, dance-derived acts like the Prodigy. Punk bleeds into the playlists on Radio 1, the new music station that won't play anything officially old. The band that swept 1997's Brit awards, the Manic Street Preachers, started life as clones of the Clash. Punk is comic and acceptable, purged of its original gob and germs and homemade Oxfam elements. People love it because it's like the *Beano*. The present-day Buzzcocks and Sex Pistols look like they were designed by someone who draws for the *Beano*. But then sometimes I feel that way myself, when I look in the mirror.

Living in Manchester, though, you wouldn't immediately notice any of that. Walk around Manchester and you walk around a city that has consciously and carefully avoided retrospective references to punk because of the strength of dance music and club culture. Youth fashion has been derived from sports and leisurewear for over a decade; Manchester has its own indigenous designers and outlets, too. There is a Manchester look. Not elegant, I'd say, and certainly not cheap. But characteristic of the place. If we are to talk about the late twentieth century in Britain, then Manchester first of all has to be recognized (and has been) as a city with a mind of its own. Manchester's current status as a late-twentieth-century city, an international city, a 'post-modern' city, or whatever you want to call it, began with punk.

Manchester is good at wiping away the past and emphasizing its newness. The manufacturing history of cities like Manchester has meant that an object like a factory is not necessarily a thing to be revered. We knock down old mills unless someone's got a radical reason for refurbishing them, and then we celebrate the difference. Manchester's version of leisure is an industry in itself, perpetual but very much live-for-today, as the throngs drink the night away in the basement of the old Watts Warehouse, once the biggest Victorian textile display house and warehouse in the city and now the Britannia Hotel; as a completely different crowd head down Whitworth Street West, towards Castlefield and Deansgate, under 100-year-old railway bridges, where smart bars like Nowhere and Atlas do a brisk trade, and lights burn late in the offices of Red Alert Music and the Boardwalk nightclub, in buildings that were originally Victorian shops and schools. Although nobody cares, and nobody cared much in the late 1800s when the Victorians knocked down the old habitations of Alport, which had been standing since medieval times. And of course, under that lot somewhere is the remains of the old Roman fort and *vicus*, still incompletely excavated. But, if it ever is, and if the *Manchester Evening News* has anything to do with it, as their front page story of February 15, 1997 reflected, it'll be the 'treasure' element that will interest people the most. Not bricks and mortar.

Punk in Manchester followed that pattern of instantaneousness and same-day usefulness. Money, investment wasn't evident, making space, buildings, places to go, things to buy, almost entirely second-hand and grimy and limited. Everything under-went a brief period of being reinvented, re-used, and finally burnt out. Punk in Manchester had a working-class edge (Slaughter & The Dogs, The Drones, The Worst) that was always so dumb as to verge on the absurd; a fitting comp-lement to the conscious absurdity of more middle-class acts like the Buzzcocks, whose sexual self-absorption and humour summed up a pop sensibility enveloped in kitsch and self-parody. There were other early punk outfits who hung on with desperation to the influence of glam, like V2; and V2 later had a part to play in the rise of Joy Division via their drummer, Steve Brotherdale, who played for Warsaw, Joy Division's earlier incarnation. It's no coincidence that some of the most important early punk clubs in Manchester had kitsch connotations; The Ranch, for instance, was part of Foo Foo's Palace on Dale Street, which was, still is, the home of the hen party, hosted by the club-owning drag queen Frank Lammarr (a filthy Manchester version of Danny La Rue). The Electric Circus was surrounded by dodgy pubs and bars staging low-brow country and western acts. Rafters, on Oxford Street, was the basement of a huge cabaret nightclub. The clubs, the places, came and went. The campness fed back into punk.

Punk in Manchester exploded very quickly. Records like Ed Banger and The Nose Bleeds' *Ain't Bin To No Music School* on Tosh Ryan's Rabid label, and the Buzzcocks' first EP on Richard Boon's label, New Hormones, were a form of purgation, and were difficult to follow up. Bands changed line-up – Howard Devoto left the Buzzcocks and formed Magazine. The big labels swooped down: the Buzzcocks went to United Artists, Slaughter and the Dogs signed to Decca. The same thing happened to print. Early Mancunian punk fanzines, like Paul Morley's *Girl Trouble*, Steve Shy's *Shy Talk*, and Mick Middles' *Ghast Up*, were only viable between the second half of 1976 and autumn 1977. After that, punk was a national obsession.

But whereas in other parts of the country it's arguable that punk 'unfolded' – in the manner argued by Stewart Home in his 1995 book *Cranked Up Really High* (a title paying tribute to Slaughter & The Dogs' single of that name) – punk in Manchester was somewhat sidelined. This doesn't mean to say it wasn't there any more. It's just that other things happened which obscured our awareness of Manchester punk. First, though, let's look at Home's argument about punk because it's important. He traces what he calls 'true punk' in Britain, Europe and America, from the seventies to the nineties, from early 'ideological' punk of the sort I've been mentioning, to Oi! bands like the Exploited and GBH, to 'white power rock & roll' of the objectionable, fascist sort played by Skrewdriver and the 4 Skins, to gender-punk – the female Riot Grrl bands of the early part of this decade such as Huggy Bear and Bikini Kill. This 'unfolding' certainly included Manchester: Oi! bands like Blitz emerged from the city in 1980–81 and had a big following; the Nazi group Skrewdriver, who originated in Blackpool, were based in Manchester at one point and released records on a local label. And Huggy Bear got themselves a Mancunian manager, Liz Naylor, ex-editor of *City Fun* fanzine.

No, the reason true punk, 'ideological punk', didn't occupy centre stage for very long in Manchester was The Fall. Mark E. Smith's abrasion of the English language is a commentary on England itself; the name 'The Fall' seemed at first to suggest a throwback to Blake and his *döppelganger* homeland; industrial hell on the one side, hallucinatory Albion on the other. Seeing them for the first time in 1977 provided deeper focus: their songs provided a soundtrack for the mind for the following year, exploring parts of Manchester for the first time, the wrecked parts, the parts with a past, north of the centre, Cheetham Hill, empty synagogues in the snow. But the point is, Smith was there. Anti-intellectual, well that's nothing new in

Manchester, but he doesn't claim common grassroots support either. The Fall weren't at all a subcultural phenomenon. They wore the wrong clothes, were familiar with esoterica, the kabala, occultism as a state of mind created by place. They remain frightening without being theatrical. At the time, they made punk rock groups look like jumping puppets. I don't think Joy Division would have happened without the Fall, because the Fall made it possible for musicians in Manchester to think of themselves as artists, as doing an act of art.

Snapshot: Sunday, February 25, 1979
The television set in the Gaythorn pub is tuned to ITV, but five males huddled around one particular table are obviously not watching, for their conversation is being monitored by an ancient cassette tape-recorder, spattered in white emulsion from an overenthusiastic bout of home decorating. The electric-lit jaundice yellow of the pub interior stands out luridly against the outer darkness of Albion Street. We'd met at seven as arranged, over the road in Little Peter St, inside a building occupied by Tony Davidson, whose TJM label releases songs by bands like the Distractions. These and others rent out the ramshackle rooms in the building as rehearsal space. The walls of Room 6, covered in harsh graffiti, contain Joy Division's equipment. I'd walked in, meeting the eyes of their manager Rob Gretton, bullet-headed, bespectacled, ironically bullying, enthusiastic. The band had been running through their material, the prelude to me interviewing them; a much-relished but somewhat frightening job I was doing for the fortnightly magazine *New Manchester Review*. When the time came, only three of the band went to the Gaythorn: along with

Rob Gretton there trudged Ian Curtis, Steve Morris, and Peter Hook. Barney Sumner had other things to do, I can't remember what.

The approach I took to interviews at that time was consciously, ridiculously unstructured. I didn't ask plain, simple questions. The plain, simple questions went clean out of my head every time. Instead I liked to allow a casual conversation about any subject to develop, into which I could drop the odd, incredibly complex, usually very introverted remark, which interviewees would have to fathom. I took it all very personally. I was also quite reserved. One of the group may have sensed this, for he seemed hostile at the time. Peter Hook said almost nothing throughout, but tapped out the tension in proto-morse code on the glass ashtray on the table in front of us.

At one point I say to them, 'I get the feeling there is a shell sometimes that I can't penetrate somehow, or maybe I'm reacting to the way other people see you.' Asked by Gretton to explain what I mean, I start recalling the last time I saw Joy Division, a fortnight previously, at the Russell Club. 'There were a proportion of people who came to see you after the article in the *NME*. And there were a proportion of people who were dedicated fans. And there were a proportion of people who are regular visitors to the Russell Club, and they stood at the back drinking. And the ones who came to see you stood at the front. And what I noticed was, no one wanted to look at each other. And there seemed to be this underlying conflict in the audience, this three-way conflict. What I'm trying to suggest is, is that the kind of effect you're trying to create?'

'What is it you mean?' says Morris, 'How?'

'By doing what you do.'

'Alienating the audience?' Gretton suggests. 'From what I'd say,' he continues, 'I'm not in the band, I'm in the audience, but I'd say they play regardless of the audience. They're just playing for themselves.'

Gretton has become Gretton again, he is protecting them; they might as well have stayed in the rehearsal room, no need for audiences, no need for the group to talk to journalists. 'That's why he doesn't say much on stage,' Gretton nods in the direction of Ian Curtis.

Then Curtis, who has been listening carefully to this anxious game of verbal footsie, ventures his opinion: 'No one's told them how to react. Some of the stuff is testing the audience. Testing their reactions.'

This is what I wanted to hear, the talk of unmapped territory.

The danger at the time was definition, in being defined. My cautiousness, my suspicions, were aroused, by the bland assumption, made mostly by London journalists, that Manchester had a coherent music 'scene'. In view of this, many words were written, by many writers, concerning the fragmentedness of Manchester's music, the disjunct emotion and argumentative sound, literally, of so much that was going on, even when it was supposedly co-operative. You went, for example, to the Manchester Musicians Collective, at Band on the Wall once a week, and maybe you joined a band. But the bands were forever falling out, stabbing each other in the back, and being unbearable, as well as making unbearable music. There was also considerable resentment at the inadequacy of the London-based press speaking on behalf of a separate, distant northern city. In an interview with the people behind the then-latest Manchester fanzine, *City Fun*, in publication since late 1978, writer and sometime manager of the Distractions, Martin X, told me: 'What you must understand is we're not in competition with any magazine except *NME* and *Sounds*. 'Cause all they say is what their writers think. They don't find out what a band was like. They never ask the audience.'

However, there was another danger in being defined, and described, and colonized by the London press, even when it was ex-Mancunians like Paul Morley who were doing the writing. And that lay in the suspicion that the argument hadn't been drawn out to its logical conclusion: that all those nights spent in every one of those stinking, decrepit, unsafe, desperate venues that existed in and around the city at that time, were leading towards something that involved audiences and performers (who had, as individuals, sprung from audiences). This experience was one of a continuing debate, and not just because, when punk bands started playing, people had picked up a habit of heckling them, the bands replying in kind. This was often hilarious, but seldom amounted to constructive conversation. The real debate existed in the nature of the nights you were living through and the relationships with people you knew and the knowledge that you were all contributing something, to the babble, because occasionally, every so often, everything would seem to come into focus and everything would seem to make sense, and we would seem to be getting somewhere. No one knew quite where. But Joy Division defined that movement into the unknown.

Much of the conversation with Joy Division that Sunday

night revolved around this need to avoid the deadening effect of London journalistic reification. Morris mentions the failure of the latest media hype: power pop. The remark is meant to embarrass me: *New Manchester Review*'s founder, Andrew Jaspan, manages a power pop band called the Smirks, who have a contract with Jonathan Richman's Beserkeley label. The Smirks are what their name suggests: smiling, good-time, nice blokes, pro musicians. The *Review* has a concordant reputation: an events magazine with features, put together by a core group of professional journalists, a magazine that's so consciously well-meaning and middle-class that it constantly fails to grasp the point of what is going on around it. In my deluded fashion I believe I can change that, by arguing against the easy answer, and to their credit, Jaspan and co run interviews like this one with Joy Division. I wasn't the first on the *Review* to affect this approach: Paul Morley had previously written for the fortnightly, as had Howard Devoto. Then they both got too busy to carry on.

Joy Division therefore represented a very *hopeful* strand in culture at the beginning of 1979. They seemed to bear this out, that night at the Gaythorn, by talking optimistically about the future, highlighting at the same time their sense of difference from others. 'I don't think there's anyone to compare us to,' says Curtis. 'Everyone ignored us ... I'd rather not be part of anything.' Then Morris adds, 'Whatever we do from now till whenever, it's always going to be expanding.' I ask them to describe their notion of expansion in more detail, and then, from outside, in what might be a melodramatic touch straight out of a Hammer horror film, a bell starts to toll. The Town Hall clock, booming out the time: ten. Ian carries on: 'The way the Pop Group use echo on stage ... that is a new thing. There's various possibilities of using techniques like that in studios, maybe not now because we're not experienced enough ... but in the next couple of years. There's other things like disco – I quite like disco. The way German disco is arranged, there's a lot of things you could take from that. The way the vocals are tweaked, there's such a lot that you'd like to do ... two years ago, I'd've liked to do what we're doing now, but we just couldn't play.'

Ian isn't alone in expressing some interest in disco. Rob Gretton also mentions it, a little later. 'Music's all about snobbery,' he says. 'That's what that article was about in *Melody Maker* two weeks ago, that I told you all to read. Did you read it? It didn't look like an interesting article. Disco and all that. But it was saying that people *need* to be told what to like, that this is a hip thing to like. And maybe they'll like it or like the opposite.' He's educating his boys, at this point, bringing them on. Everything is suspect. The business, the music, the mind of the audience. At the same time, it's all malleable, and therefore all possibilities are open.

That night at the Russell Club two weeks previously had been the fourth time I'd seen Joy Division. It was unsettling, not just because of the effect I'd felt of a shell around them, and of an 'alienated audience'. Those things I considered positive; but that night I'd also seen Ian drinking heavily and during his ensuing performance he blacked out and fell off the stage. The Russell Club itself wasn't conducive to feeling relaxed. I was knocked unconscious, hit on the head from behind

with a Newcastle Brown bottle, there on the dancefloor one
night by a pack of patriotic off-duty soldiers, during a Wayne
County gig. At the Russell I'd also seen an entire audience
of skinheads and punks watching Penetration suddenly split
and turn and change for no obvious reason into a kicking,
punching, stabbing riot. Joy Division were not a punk band;
they belonged to a subsequent phase, in which snobbery and
elitism, as Gretton defined, played a certain part, especially
among those who professed to liking them. If their music
contained violence it was in the extent to which they took
risks in performing; creating, externalizing this stuff in front of
a line of eyewitnesses.

The risk-taking had seemed foolhardy at first, in 1978.
They had been dressed in black motorbike leather at the
Manchester leg of the Stiff Test/Chiswick Challenge, a talent-
spotting night which the two aforementioned London independent labels were touring around the country. Joy Division,
who had recently changed their name from Warsaw, arrived
late at the venue, Rafters, on Oxford Street. The promoters,
New Manchester Review, refused to let them play. Harsh words
were exchanged. Joy Division were allowed on last, for a
mere 20 minutes, and were excluded from the talent-spotting
competition. They wore big leather bike-boots. They were
unsmiling and aggressive and their songs, taken from their
first EP, *An Ideal For Living*, set them apart from everyone
else on the bill. And I don't remember who else was on the
bill, other than the fact that every band seemed unremittingly,
unapologetically to have still been playing pub rock: happy,
positive, jumping up and down. Afterwards, putting my records
away in the DJ booth, I met Rob Gretton, raving about the

brilliance of that last group. Above the noise of bouncers telling us all to clear out, I remember agreeing. Then Rob told me he was going to manage Joy Division.

In another pub interview in the winter of 1980 Tony Wilson described to me the beginnings of Factory: 'We recorded something with Durutti Column. In August (1978) we got a phone call from Roger Eagle. So I drove over to Liverpool. I sat down with Roger and Pete (Fulwell) and they said, 'Right, do a twelve-inch single with four bands on'. So I said, no, do a double seven-inch. I got back in the car, I drove back, I said to Alan (Erasmus), they don't wanna do what I wanna do, I don't wanna do what they wanna do. Why don't we do it? About that point Alan Wise and Nigel Bagley were getting involved at the Factory. The club was drifting away from us, we weren't too bothered about it. This is October. Also September there'd been the thing with Durutti Column, when I'd asked Martin (Hannett) to go into the studio with these tapes they'd done in July and see what he could do with mixing them. And we just mixed the tracks and put the tracks out, as part of this record. I also asked Rob, do you wanna put a couple of Joy Division tracks on and he said yeah. And Martin did that at Cargo, which was 'Digital' and 'Glass'. And (John) Dowie did three tracks. On a four-side thing you can afford a comedy break. And then the Cabs (Cabaret Voltaire) did two tracks. And (Peter) Saville designed the sleeve. And basically that was it, *A Factory Sample*.'

The story of Wilson's fruitless Liverpool schlep brought to mind tantalizing thoughts of a kind of Manchester–Liverpool alliance involving Roger Eagle and Pete Fulwell, who ran

Eric's club on Mathew Street. Further Manchester–Liverpool cross-fertilization had almost happened between Factory and Zoo Records, and they even organized an open-air festival in August 1979, at Leigh, in between the two cities. Zoo gave the world the Teardrop Explodes and Echo and the Bunnymen. Still with us, more or less, in the late nineties: the Bunnymen reformed in 1997 and released new, immediately praised material, and Julian Cope is still playing and being the loveable eccentric. But Joy Division metamorphosed into something else. As an early Factory press release said, *We sell flesh and vinyl.* Ian Curtis's death, followed by the success of *Closer*, marked the point where Factory became the musical establishment in Manchester. But it also marked the point where Joy Division's surviving members immersed themselves in the sound of dance music. And Ian Curtis had seen that much coming.

Despite the fact that Joy Division weren't destined to last, and that they were fated to become some other design, some other sound, we are still having to deal with them. We are still having to talk about them. It's obvious Manchester wouldn't have had much of a music business without them. It's also obvious Manchester wouldn't have had the Haçienda without them, and that Manchester wouldn't have the kind of heritage industry it's now capable of cashing in on, as the millenium turns. What really fascinates, though, is the Joy Division moment, the meshing of individual tensions in enclosed spaces over short timespans. The way that combined tension evolved. *The time of becoming.* Maybe that's how we should talk about Joy Division and Manchester.

Part One

1

The Headmaster Ritual

'Y'know, you're me best mate, you are [*hic, belch*].' In any laddish TV comedy of the nineties, there always comes a moment when one bibulous character slurs his fraternal love to another. Funny, that: in Manchester – where 'The Lad' was as ubiquitous as in any other northern city long before the media construct became fashionable – you never hear any bloke say that to a pal. Like crying in public and wearing team shirts every waking hour, it's something you'd associate with overly hysterical Geordies, not gruff Mancunians.

Nevertheless, in this city as elsewhere, the relationship between a young lad and his best mate takes second place only to the son–mother bond. Women rarely understand this, mainly because men are so brilliant at compartmentalizing their lives and keeping their mouths in check. Since no self-respecting bloke ever tells the unvarnished truth in mixed company, unless he's gay, it would come as a shock to most women to hear how men rank the importance of nurturing different kinds of relationships. As a facetious friend once remarked, echoing Kipling: 'A woman can be a wife but a bloke can be a *best mate.*'

Mrs Thatcher was obviously wrong in her notorious assertion that 'There is no such thing as society; there are families and there are individual men and women.' Wrong, at least in the case of the society which produced the stories in this book. Substitute 'there are blokes, their best mates and their gangs' and you'd have a better tool for dissection in two cultural areas for which the Manchester of the eighties and nineties is rightly celebrated – football and pop. Women, at least in the shapes of wives and girlfriends, barely register as forces of influence. As prime actors, they are wholly negligible. Women as mothers, of course, is a quite separate business; indeed, the development of Oasis in particular was markedly shaped by matriarchal power. But then Manchester is a city dominated by the social patterns of immigrant cultures – the Irish variant of martyred mothers and difficult, estranged fathers being a common one. What this is leading to is an apology of sorts for the fact that all the voices you will hear are male and that the events are powered by testosterone rather than oestrogen, with women making only fleeting appearances. One exception provides ironic counterpoint: that the *NME* reviewer who gave Oasis such a big initial break in print should have been female; an unwitting midwife to the band's pivotal role in the legitimization and popularization of 'New Laddism'.

The first mistake made by many when examining Oasis is to bill it as, fundamentally, a story about two brothers. (Or, if you're Paul Gallagher, of two-and-a-half brothers.) At root, Oasis begins with not two brothers but two best mates: Chris Hutton and Paul 'Guigsy' McGuigan. The latter is now a metropolitan multimillionaire, enjoying the cushiest job any band-member can have (namely plodding bassist) and able to summon up the delights of which he once adolescently dreamt. The former remains in Manchester's suburbia, working long factory hours, his teenage fantasies long since consigned to a far corner of his memory.

They are no longer best mates, to say the least. The conception of the group Oasis sprang from these two boyhood friends' imaginations; the final realization, however, depended on that friendship's brutal betrayal. Only then does Oasis become a fraternal construction – one ironically founded on a kind of fratricide.

There are two great watersheds in the course of 'best mates' lives: leaving primary school at the age of 11, then leaving education altogether somewhere between 16 and 18. (In the milieu of this book, the minority who go to university at 18 don't count.) There's always the kids 'round our way' who remain acquaintances over the years but usually the binding agent of a school's regime trumps sharing a postcode. Just as army induction unites the poor bloody infantry against the Regimental Sergeant-Major, other platoons and other services (the foreign opposition coming a poor fourth), the common enemy of Establishment, other classes' gangs and other schools cements adolescent individuals into a tribal unit.

Generally, no one cares about the pre-pubes one leaves behind at junior school. If intensity of shared experience is what heightens the value of a friendship, then nothing you do at juniors' is going to match the searing stuff secondary has to offer. First tingling-willy-going-up-a-gym-rope versus first shag; first fist-fight versus first knife-fight; first taste of a tab (Benson's) versus first taste of a tab (acid): it's never a serious contest. So, at least in Manchester's working classes, the choices of mates you make at 11 or 12 are among the most vital you'll ever make. Those lads, the interests and rites of passage you'll share, essentially shape the bloke you'll become as much as any genetic inheritance.

In some ways, it's as frighteningly random a selection process as the dreaded 11-plus which would toss you onto the scrapheap before you'd even started. Over at St Mark's secondary back in 1978, Noel Gallagher had discovered this for himself, mistakenly ending up amidst a collection of stiffs and squits from whose clutches it took several seemingly endless terms to escape. A certain anti-intellectualism, austere self-sufficiency and caution have clung to him since.

Chris Hutton and Guigsy were luckier: they found each other, then chose their boys well. If Burnage High didn't exactly bring years of fabulous enlightenment and joy to Chris and Guigs – indeed, schools like that were seemingly designed to do quite the opposite – then at least neither would leave with the kind of visible spiritual scars inflicted upon Noel or his predecessor as the city's bard, Morrissey. Burnage High was not a 'Headmaster Ritual' archetype; the sadists tended to be in the playground rather than the staffroom.

The school, like Burnage itself, was unknown outside Manchester. (Unknown outside Burnage, alleged Longsight's loyalists.) Infamy lay just around the corner. Yet even today, it's a slightly strange trip from city centre into Burnage. Coming off the roundabout down the arterial Kingsway, you'd never know you have entered a discrete community. Discreet also: quiet, unprepossessing, and surrounded by louder, better-known locales such as Longsight, Moss Side and Stockport, its modesty did not rub off on its most famous sons. There's a distinct whiff of respectability and upward mobility in parts too – especially if you've just ventured in from Levenshulme or Longsight's more down-at-heel zones. Burnage's rougher end, where council properties dominate instead of owner-occupiers, never instils the same fear and loathing as Moss Side's counterpart a short drive to the west.

The Gallaghers might have lived on the wrong side of Burnage's tracks, whilst Chris and Guigsy resided 'uptown', but compared to the polar extremes possible in Manchester, such distinctions are of small degree. As a sociologist would tell you, separating out the C2s from the C1s and DEs can be tricky, especially in such socially mobile times. Quite healthily, an outsider would simply dub the entire area upper working class and leave the pettier snobberies alone. No one in the Oasis story was ever as badly off as, say, the slum-dwelling young Ringo Starr, nor as resolutely bourgeois as Damon Albarn. Those who set such great store by these things – and there are plenty of self-loathing middle-class types and chip-on-shoulder proles in the music media who do – are entitled to trumpet Oasis as 'a working class band.'

By 1982, when Chris and Guigs started at Burnage High, the seventies were not merely factually finished but emotionally so too. Ian Curtis was dead, the Buzzcocks split and the Jam teetering on the edge of a Weller-made abyss. The savagely deflationary 1981 Budget had definitively established the monetarist terror. And, in Manchester, as casuals replaced scarved hooligans on the terraces, City had surrendered their supposed top dog role to Atkinson's United. The eighties may have meant Filofaxes, champagne and stock options to the South but to Mancunians it offered only economic depression and social disintegration, and a soundtrack to match. Chris and Guigs were of the Smiths generation: their start and finish dates at school exactly bookended the career of the city's standard-bearers. Morrissey would always be accused of being teenager-fixated in his lyrics, a twenty-something obsessed with reliving the ignominies of youth – but of course, to lads like Chris and

Guigs, he was speaking directly, no matter what his age. And the fact that the guitarist was self-evidently the hippest man in town didn't hinder the Smiths' appeal either.

Chris Hutton was always an uncomplicated kind of guy: a classic 'English Mancunian' with a stable family, a good, respectable home and the decent values of loyalty and honesty that go down well in a classroom. Always one of the lads, he preserved a sense of self too, keen to look for the better buzz in life, ready to step back and do his own thing if necessary. In that, he found common cause with Guigs, the boy he sat next to in many subject classes. Still, Guigs was a little harder to fathom.

An Ulster Protestant background, an ailing father a year from death, a highly intelligent and influential mother and a calculating, observational nature combined to make Guigsy a touch unusual; not quite the bantering, messing, don't-give-a-shit lad norm. When you hear about how Guigs acts within Oasis, you recognize him from his youth: watching, assessing, intervening at the right moments, always preserving his position and holding the balance of power. He was certainly one of the clever sods at school, for which Chris remained grateful throughout as the cribsheets and whispered asides flew thick and fast.

Chris, like 99 per cent of the kids dumped into Manchester's shittier schools, soon decided that academia was boring and that books were the tools of the enemy. Guigs survived by being intellectually generous and keeping any swottish sensibilities in check. The imaginative tendencies that might elsewhere have flowered in English composition were diverted into the art of bullshitting and yarn-spinning, at which Guigsy excelled. As Noel over at St Marks also discovered, the suspiciously smart can always escape ostracism by being entertaining – and Guigsy's stories about George Best and his dad, whatever their truthfulness, kept the gullible open-mouthed and happy. Besides, both he and Chris were always up for a game of football, an attribute that can excuse almost anything else, especially in Manchester.

Latent artistry would emerge later, in lyrics and music, although Chris had already given an indication of what he had to offer when he was reluctantly press-ganged into a school choir. He knew he had a good voice at 12, with a physique and look perfect for a frontman already apparent, but for now sport was all that mattered. If the lads weren't playing football, they'd be on the cricket pitch. If Chris wasn't jibbing up to Old Trafford to see the Reds, then it'd be to watch Lancashire with Guigs and CJ, a Levenshulme lad. Inseparable chums in all but one respect: if United were at home on a Saturday, Chris would be there with his dad, leaving Guigs at home with Piccadilly Radio.

For McGuigan had chosen to buck the trans-Irish Sea norm and support Manchester City instead, like his father before him. Usually, only the most militant of Loyalists from Belfast would prefer City to United. The tradition, embodied by Best and Whiteside, is that United are an island-of-Ireland side, despite their Catholic foundation. Years on, when 'not supporting United' would be the kind of C.V. entry that'd help you remain in a Gallagher-run band, the choice looked inspired.

Chris was hopelessly hooked on United by the time he was 13, an obsession from which only poverty would forcibly release him in 1990. And who could blame him? Atkinson's United were coming to a peak, winning two FA Cups and joining most title chases with a brand of wing-driven flair-footie which Reds had craved since Docherty's departure. More than that: Old Trafford in the eighties truly deserved the 'Theatre of Dreams' marketing bull which it so patently does not today. The game still belonged to the young, male working classes, with United offering blokes exciting promotions to the Stretford End, United Road Paddock and, much later, to the growling beast of K-Stand. Football introduces a lad to the power and spirit of mass intoxication long before music can. Those who later yearn for centre-stage themselves are often virally infected by witnessing football idolatry first. Indeed, in many ways, pop never catches up with football – the occasional Spike Island or Knebworth cannot add up to what 55,000 *every fortnight* at Old Trafford induces in a lad. Only the fact that music can cast a spell on the individual, alone with his bedroom tape-deck and first faltering lyrics, keeps pop in the running.

Guigsy, meanwhile, talked a better game than he was entitled to. He'd plumped for City at their nadir and unsurprisingly did not share Chris's match-going compulsion to the same extent. Sure, he went to Maine Road every now and then – certainly more often than Liam was managing at the time – but dropping to the Second Division did not inspire him in the way it did Noel. Whilst Noel took perverse pleasure from his one, 'proper', season as a City supporter, Guigsy was happy enough with his radio commentators and 'Pink' final scores editions. (There's no shame in this. It's quite normal for kids to be taken by expectant dads to Maine Road and for them to run out screaming 'Never take me to that shit-hole nightmare again.')

Guigsy's natural fluency made up for his absentee-ism: football gossip and banter was the main classroom currency and Guigsy always held his own. The subject of football in general united the lads more than their specific loyalties divided them; or at least until such time as they might have to start fighting each other at derbies. Guigsy's stories now included his classic 'George Best Taught Me Football', which everyone in the Oasis camp would hear several times over the years. He diversified into boxing. The current tabloid hero was Barry McGuigan, and the happy congruence of surname meant that Burnage High soon thrilled to Ulster stories woven by his 'close second cousin' Paul.

Nobody really cared whether the Guigsy homestead genuinely used to welcome Barry and George round for a cup of tea and a bottle of scotch; the blarney was good, whiling away classroom – or, later, tour-bus –

hours of boredom. Chris would laugh at his mate's shaggy-doggery, shake his grinning head and tell him 'you're on top, you are', but never indulged himself.

There were other lads to knock about with too: a kid called Tony French, for example, who accompanied them on a roaring first-year trip to Amsterdam where they all learned more about life than they should have. Good with a felt-tip and pencil was Tony, forever drawing logos and designs on his exercise books – later, he'd become the designer for Oasis. Then there were the Shenton brothers, Mark and Steve, living a few doors down from Chris. At various times they were respective best mates of two 'Irish' scallies with minor reputations around Burnage – Liam and Noel Gallagher. Being 'Irish' (i.e. Catholic), they attended St Mark's (rather than Burnage High), a semi-respectable institution which offered the added bonus of allowing girls to attend.

Chris only knew Noel from the odd sighting around Mr Sifters record shop in Burnage; an apparently lost and serious soul dressed in whatever old youth-cult garb he fancied that month, a study in post-modern confusion. Liam, being virtually Chris's age, seemed the more visible. 'Will', as he was always known then, was more your face-around-town, already carrying a certain swagger and attitude. Behind his back, they'd call him 'Make-Up Face', testifying to the amusing eyeliner effect of his heavy brows and colouring which would later be so adored. Of the interests for which he is now famed – football, music and women – only the last applied back then: the City boys Chris knew had never seen Liam at a match during that era, whilst the Sifters regulars simply didn't know him. But the girls who traipsed up to the Gallaghers' door every morning, asking if Will was walking into school, certainly knew him.

Until you hit puberty, football is all. It is hard to overemphasize the game's centrality in Manchester. The chattering classes who've swallowed the myth that the world deserted football in the eighties, only returning after Italia '90 and *Fever Pitch*, never grasp the game's dominance in the North. Football never went out of style or fashion: indeed, in the eighties, a football stadium was the only place to be for the lad-about-town on a Saturday. Dressing smart and casual may have been deemed worthwhile *per se* but its ultimate purpose was to make you look the part in the Kippax stand or Stretford End. Similarly, the ridiculous media construction of the 'New Lad' circa 1992–3 meant nothing up North: the Lad himself was not subject to style or analysis – he just *was*. 'New Man' in a Mancunian context could only ever mean an incoming transfer.

A lad's pubertal obsession with the growth and performance of his trouser-snake seems directly linked to his increasing awareness of music – and, by extension, of the attendant trappings of youth culture. Oh, and of women too, of course. Football then has challengers for its place as the pre-eminent bonding agent and

prime topic of discussion – although such is its established dominance, it seeps easily into adjacent areas
like clothes. And henceforth, the era of 'playing out'
is replaced by 'hanging out'. These can be tough times
for those who can't get with the programme, since
nothing is ever stated explicitly at that age. There
is no divide quite like that between the teenager
who's discovered wanking and all that follows, and
the lad who hasn't. The cruellest thing Chris saw as
a 12-year-old wasn't some physical violence but the
following. A mate who'd hit puberty over the summer,
and who subconsciously understood everything this
entailed, answered the door at the start of a new term
to the kid who'd been his best schoolmate the previous
year. Said kid, however, was still pissing through a
mini-roll rather than a frankfurter. The kid goes 'Are
you playing out?', just as he always did. Complete
mortification all round. *'Playing out?!?'* Chris's mate
simply closed the door on him without a word and
never spoke to him again. Neither of them had to
say anything and probably couldn't have explained
the thinking behind it anyway. His next muttered
comment – 'Let's open Mum's Freemans catalogue'
– actually spoke volumes.

Hanging out was then the night-time agenda for
Chris and his mates, that and looking for girls, smarten-
ing up, exerting territorial dominance and generally
being men instead of boys. Football still mattered,
hugely, but innocent discussions about 'your heroes'
and how to volley were less in evidence; football was

no longer about one's consumption of the game but one's participation in it as a supporter, whether as a fighter or singer. Blue–Red rivalries mattered more now as, the older you got, you began to realize what people have done in the streets and stadia of Europe for those colours. Once you take in the understanding that comes with puberty, there are no excuses. You have to know the score on everything now or you're out.

When you're at that age, when your own self-esteem and the respect of others feel like life-or-death issues, you feel you can't opt out of the game. You're either going to be one of the boys, or a loser. And, at least until the arrival of the computer industry, once you were branded the latter, that always threatened to be that for the rest of your life. Isn't this the dynamic underpinning teenagerhood, the force that drives people in search of the latest, coolest and most dangerous?

2

Rusholme Ruffians

'Hanging Out In West Point': it could've been the title of The Rain's first album. West Point isn't really a locale as such, just a place to hang between Burnage and Levenshulme – more a state of mind than anything. As Chris and Guigs approached 13, they began to hear tales, urban legends perhaps, of the West Point Boys. If not quite a 'firm' in the footballing sense, they nonetheless became attached to stories of brawling and punch-ups which the lads would hear snatches of in the schoolyard. West Point drew its adherents from both sides of the border. Consequently, a Burnage lad hanging with the West Pointers could find himself in a ruck with the Burnage Boys, some of whom would be living across the street.

The whole area was riddled with divided loyalties, a community confused by fault-lines cutting across the usual class divides. A lad could be categorized by school, and therefore religion; by race, bearing in mind the large ethnic minority presence at Burnage High;

by football team, with Blues outnumbering Reds; and by 'gang', which as we've seen was not necessarily dictated by your home's geographical position. So any lad could find himself in a bundle for an alarmingly wide variety of reasons. As Liam would doubtless point out in defence of his own continuing brawling tendencies, where he came from it always paid to be prepared. Sometimes, pre-emptive first strikes were the only sane choice.

Chris and Guigs gravitated towards West Point for good reason: Chris had fallen out with the Burnage Boys big-style. A fair fight between Chris and a gang 'face' at the Burnage fair had still resulted in bad blood. Later, when Chris and mates were attending a party in Burnage, the local Boys mounted an attack. Joining up with West Point was both a necessity and a happy coincidence, for it was there that they regularly encountered Paul Arthurs a.k.a. Bonehead.

The great value of hanging out was that you got to schmooze with the real lads, hard men in their late teens or even twenties who had some good blarney and a bit of form to respect. Bonehead seemed hard, especially when set next to his comrades Jimmy Reagan and Pat Moran, a tight little firm-within-a-firm. And Bonehead was a Red too, if not much of a match-goer. Add the fact that he'd left school back in '81, and was therefore a man of the world, and he had Chris's respect from the off. Sometimes they'd see him away from West Point during the day, lugging a keyboard or guitar around Burnage. Someone had indeed remarked that Bonehead was a 'bit of a muso', not that this meant anything to the boys at that stage. But it would one day, of course.

The boys spent more and more time mooching about town, getting their faces known, making new contacts, investigating females, necking illicit beverages . . . the usual urban teenage existence. Guigsy, however, would sometimes go weeks without emerging from his home. Chris knew his dad's death, when he was only twelve, had hit him harder than he let on but it would be some time before he grasped the extent of the depressions that could strike Guigsy. And Guigs was never as much of a skirt-chaser as some in the gang; he wasn't the centre-of-attention kind of guy that prospers in urban beaver patrols.

Unlike Liam, of course. 'Will' was simply never in and Chris seemed to run into him and Shenton every week, despite the fact that they inhabited entirely different social circles. Cringle's Fields Fair regularly witnessed the slightly strange ritual when Liam and Chris met. For some reason Chris never understood, the two were always suspicious of each other, never quite seeing eye-to-eye. Sure, they'd always let on to each other, small-talk about this and that, check out mutual acquaintances; but they were always circling each other animalistically, keeping their guard up, chins jutting forward in the classic give-no-inch Mancunian stance.

The whimsical might say they'd seen their futures.

And in hindsight, like Sherlock Holmes and the curiously non-barking dog, Chris notices how remarkable were the two subjects he *never* remembers hearing Liam discuss: music and football. What he would talk about was women, the most desirable of whom Liam would award a special accolade that helps explain his choice of wife. When, for example, he saw Chris's girlfriend, he yelped, 'Fit as a fookin' film star! She's a fookin' film star, I'm tellin' ya!' And who knows; perhaps Patsy as a little girl used to simper, 'Ooh, he's as hunky as a pop star.'

By the time Chris and Guigsy got into upper school, at least nominally on track for GCEs and CSEs, they'd built their own replica of the West Pointers inside Burnage High: a good 20 heads, self-dubbed the Chip Barm Boys – on account of their lunchtime menu choice. Not, perhaps, a name as calculated to inspire fear as, say, the Urmston Razor Squad or the Chelsea Headhunters. (What were they going to do, smear their victims with margarine-soaked half-barms?) But they were a handy outfit, with something of an 'Under-Fives' feel to them. At a time when casuals ran football, many of whom belonging to bizarrely-monikered firms, it seemed quite congruous. Tellingly, it was an all-white outfit too.

If you wanted to demonstrate the concept of segregation to someone in the eighties, you only needed to show them around a northern inner-city comp at breaktime. Not that the Chip Barmers were card-carrying British Nationalists or anything, although

Guigsy was beginning to display alarming Thatcherite sensibilities. But in a tough school like that, defending one's identity and heritage was normal, whatever one's colour. Outsiders would often see teenagers' racially based conflict as explicitly racist, which was not always necessarily the case: sometimes, ethnicity just happened to be on hand as another difference to fight around. On another day, footballing loyalty would have sufficed. Whilst very many young Mancs in the early eighties would've used phrases such as 'Paki' or 'nigger' without a second thought, most would still have recoiled in horror from the fascist incitements of the NF.

The trouble was that in the mix of any white gang, hard-line racists found easy shields to hide behind, be they so-called 'casual' racists or non-racists who just fancied a fight. Such activities are then easily manipulated. What participants may have seen as an 'innocent' bundle becomes a 'blow for white supremacy' once *Bulldog* has reported it. Naturally, it would be preferable if no such actions took place to start with – but at Burnage High and schools like it in the grim early eighties, there was never a chance of that. And some weren't too arsed about it anyway: there's anecdotal evidence from all sides that ritualized skirmishing could be fun, in a seventies-hooligan kind of way, as hundreds of lads piled into each other without doing too much damage every break time.

The laughter died the day a lower-school white at Burnage High stabbed an Asian 13-year old to death.

Suddenly, in the media storm, the school became the latest symptom of the collapse in society's values, a symbol of what urban brutality could induce. The assailant, so it was reported around school, had fled the scene yelling 'I killed a Paki' with something akin to manic glee. Race relations at the school were never the same again, as media, police and social services swarmed around the campus. Every new school morning fizzed with tension – the upper school, where knives and general weaponry were more common currency, became the tinderbox waiting to explode. The passing of a few weeks did nothing to heal the open wounds. When an Asian upper-school kid brought in a rejigged airgun, held it to a white boy's head and said 'This one's for you', dramatic repercussions were inevitable.

The white kid phoned 'Jimmy' that night, a habitual truant and King Lad who'd been the cock of the walk and had a reputation for being the maddest for it. Here was something worth going into school for. Next morning, he cornered the gun-toter and floored him with frightening ferocity. Jimmy had once shown similar fearlessness when faced with one Noel Gallagher during a Longsight–Burnage confrontation. Despite the fact that Noel was four years older and telling him to 'do one', Jimmy's defiance provoked a small ruck that ended with Noel getting a chip barm smashed into his face. A stunned Gallagher walked away; probably a wise decision. So much for 'Chip Barm' being a name of harmless intent. Jimmy had always been one of Chris's top boys, a lad you had to respect. Never knew fear, and always took up a physical challenge from the age of 13 onwards. Getting shot in the hand by a rival gang's kid – in a scene spookily reminiscent of the film *Small Faces* – simply added to the reputation at the cost of nothing more than a few smears of blood.

By home-time, word was around: it was coming to an 'off', the flashpoint everyone had been building up to for weeks. Whites and Asians from other schools were up for it too. The forces massed on Kingsway, Burnage's main thoroughfare. Bedlam ensued. Traffic screeched to a halt in both directions as scores of lads roamed up and down the carriageway, beating the shit out of each other. Drivers started getting out of cars to have a pop too: two Asians were still down once the smoke had cleared. This was no longer just the school's problem, but the community's.

The next day, 17 white lads were called out of roll-calls and taken off to be locked away from the rest of the kids. About half of them were Chip Barm Boys, including Chris and Guigsy, although Guigsy had been somehow absent from the mass ruck the previous night. The 'Burnage 17' were going to be thrown to the wolves, namely the much-loathed local social services. A transfer to the local remedial school, Shawbrook, was on the cards, as well as a reference or two to the Police. But there were those who had more pressing business with the indicted lads.

As the 17 ate their lunch alone after the rest

of the school had gone to lessons, they began to feel something wasn't right. The dining room was glass-walled, completely open to the outside view. With mounting horror, the lads watched as dozens and dozens of Asians began to come up to the windows, making throat-slitting gestures and carrying weapons. They were surrounded by the brothers, cousins and cohorts of the upper school's Asians. One lad made a nervous crack about *Zulu* – nobody laughed.

Suddenly, seemingly within seconds, they were all inside, making good their threats. A maelstrom of chairs, tables, knives and glass swirled around the room as the hopelessly outnumbered whites ran for their lives. Somehow, they had the presence of mind to make for the tiny kitchen, barricading themselves in behind the door. As the hordes bayed for their blood outside, they managed to put a phone call through to one of the lads' dads, who was round the back of the kitchen with a van within minutes. They escaped through a back door into the van and sped off, swearing instant revenge.

They tried to exact it next day but the escalation had brought a new element – police reinforcements. Almost 100 lads had marched to the school, swelled by a white influx from St Albans school, but as soon as they launched into the Asians in the yard, the police moved in. 'Kill the Bill' went the cry from some, but the odds were now against them. The Asians survived. The Burnage 17 returned home to telephone calls informing them they'd been expelled – Chris and

Guigsy included. They'd be going to Shawbrook to do their exams and to court to defend their liberty.

In the end, the Battle of Burnage High put only three lads in the dock. Jimmy and Danny got a fine and a discharge, whilst the testimony of Chris won his mate Paddy a complete acquittal. The fact that they'd all fucked up their exams didn't bother any of them, and Guigsy still managed to pass half a dozen. More remarkably, Guigsy alone found a way to sidle back into Burnage High, returning for the new term to continue his studies. Not for the last time, Guigsy's unique self-preservation skills had seen him through where Chris's had not.

Years later, when Paolo Hewitt's Oasis book was published, Guigsy's story was 'embellished' to the extent that he was portrayed as a 'murder suspect', suspended while the police investigated the original fatal stabbing. A nice gangster-glam touch, boys. Like the T.S. Eliot cat with a knack for absenteeism was Guigsy. How did Paddy, the Chip Barm veteran put it? 'We'd come into school every morning, not giving a fuck as usual; Guigsy'd be the only one carrying a big school-bag, full of books 'n' stuff. The rest of us never owned a school-bag to start with. He'd buy a flapjack after lunch instead of saving the cash for cigs. D'yer know what I mean – he was never quite there with the rest, was he?' Indeed: Paddy knew a symbolic act when he saw one.

With Chris and Guigsy running around getting into

scrapes with both the Chip Barmers and the West Pointers, it would only be a matter of time before they'd cross Liam's path. Soon after the Burnage High affair, that night duly arrived. It was like a bad scene from *West Side Story*, except that the local gangs' memberships never had quite the sharpness of delineation enjoyed by the Sharks and Jets. Somehow Chris and Guigsy had turned up in a rival firm against Liam's; now, on a Burnage street corner at sunset, they faced each other. Naturally, Liam took the frontman's spotlight while Guigsy prowled in the bass-man's shadows, sticking close to Chris. The quarrel was archetypal: a moll from Liam's gang had been playing away with Guigsy's crowd. Loss of face, pal – whatever the century or city, the codes remain the same.

BJ was no gangster, no hard man, no cock of the school. He'd never do a runner from a ruck, but looking for mither was not his prime occupation. For Liam, it was said to be a job description. But BJ was tonight's lead-off man, the poor sod at the front of the wedge who has to take or throw the first blow – even though the alleged culprit in this contretemps was one Harvey, who'd wisely discovered a prior diary engagement.

'Where's Harvey, BJ?' spat Liam, eyes bulging within the facial contortion Fleet Street now knows so well.

'Dunno, Will,' replied BJ, truthfully.

Liam's head-butt struck dead centre. But BJ didn't go down. Not even when Liam repeated the trick. Sharp intakes all round.

'Last chance BJ – where's fookin' Harvey?'
'Dunno.'

Liam smashed into BJ for a third time. Incredibly, he barely wavered. Suddenly, BJ took two steps forward and, with the full power of his upper body behind him, crashed his head into Liam's open face. Guigsy and Chris stood transfixed as the mighty Gallagher, cock of St Marks, sprawled ingloriously across the pavement. A second's pause, like an hour: then behind them the flash of drawn blades in the dull orange light. Another night's entertainment in Burnage is well under way.

Had either Chris or Guigsy gone in on Liam at that point, the whole story of Oasis might have been very different.

3

Sweet and Tender Hooligan

When the seventies drew to a close, the colour was already slipping away from football's terraces. The sea of red, blue and white to which Old Trafford and Maine Road had become accustomed was being gradually diluted. Scarves, hats and the like were going out of fashion as fast as 'Top Trumps'. Not that we should overemphasize this development; it only applies to the cutting edge in the Stretford and Kippax, not the acrylic slacks and zip-up bomber jacket brigade in the main stands. But certainly scarf-twirling banks of colour began to fade on the terraces favoured by the more discriminating fans. The reason? The Perries were coming.

When you start generalizing in the area of football fashion, you're on dangerous ground. How can you apply blanket labels to 15,000 fans? Not *every* lad in the mid-80s United Road Paddock was a total nutter; not every person in G-stand is clinically brain dead. But it's safe to observe that the 'casual movement' which began to sweep British terraces at the turn of the decade found its greatest support in the north-west. And in Manchester the most infamous subset were the Perry Boys, who soon made their sharply cut presence felt in the Strettie. No colours as such; excellent Martin Fry haircuts; a plethora of designer labels; above all, an intense, almost Mod-like attention to image, detail and smartness. The contrast with the flared denim, tight T-shirts and excess hair of the seventies couldn't be greater.

Guigs, Chris and Bonehead were all card-carrying casuals, with Noel never quite making the mark while Liam inhabited an entirely different universe. In fact, of all the Gallaghers, Paul appeared to care the most about such matters, though he remained too second-wave mod to count. Bonehead was a proper Perry, haircut and all – these being the days when he still had a thatch, of course. For the best labels, you looked to Guigs, who always had the extra quids to spare. But for casual behaviour, Chris was your man: he had the away-game swagger, the taste for doing a bit of running about with the football lads and the ability to get stuck in when necessary.

As for the reputation of this new casual breed, Wellington's phrase about his own troops springs to mind: 'I don't know what they do to the enemy but by God, they frighten the life out of me.' The hardcore casual image was one of post-modern contradiction: clothes speaking of money, style and status in society but probably concealing the heart – and the Stanley knife – of the working-class warrior. In fact, a fighter intent on camouflaging his nature from public and police could scarcely have come up with a better disguise. In retrospect, it seems remarkable that the rest of the world took so long in catching up to what had happened.

Rival fans, of course, were totally *au fait* with every nuance of ever-changing terrace fashion. Soon, the footie/fashion cross-over had become yet another arena for tribal dispute. The most celebrated manifestation of this new culture would be *The End* zine, a more talked-about than read publication from Merseyside run by the plumbers who later became baggy band The Farm. The letters pages provided a forum for gangs of fashion-victim footie fans to air their increasingly pathetic rantings about who was wearing the hippest trainers and coolest labels as well as predictable 'who-duffed-up-whom' arguments. The only significant issue in it was 'Who started casual?' – an honour usually claimed by Scousers simply by virtue of repeating 'Arr-ay, we wuz first, like' to as many sociologists as possible.

Each club had what they thought were their own well-defined looks which changed rapidly according to the dictates of *The Face*, *i-D* et al., often resulting in a confusing congruence of style. Scousers were complaining in '83 that you couldn't tell the Mancs from the Scousers until they 'asked you the time'. If it had any significance as an era beyond establishing style as a permanent feature of the tribal rivalries, it was that it confounded all those journos and academics who were trying to make sense of football violence.

Whether you view the casual era as a golden age of football culture or a disgraceful aberration, it was certainly richly symbolic: it marked the end of the seventies, the decade that style forgot, and heralded the designer label-dominated eighties.

It is also probably fair to say that the casual scene extended the life of football hooliganism well into the eighties. It set back the authorities' attempts to counter aggro by years just at a time when they seemed to have designed an effective strategy. The sort of mass, disorganized aggro which characterized the early/mid-seventies had been struggling to stay alive since mid-1977, when the police, government and clubs began to get their act together in the wake of United's Carrow Road riot. The disappearance of colours and the coming of the casual meant more than simply changed appearances – a complete behavioural and ideological shift occurred at the end of the seventies which dictated a very different kind of aggro from shambolic scrabbling to more organized battles.

Let us be clear: no-one in Oasis was ever a *proper* hooligan in the eighties. The same applied to 95 per cent of the lads going to games. Many more might often get caught up in aggro and not be too concerned about it; such lads probably accounted for up to 20 per cent of the crowd. In that grouping you'd find Chris – the kind of lad who won't go looking for it but will have a pop and defend his colours (worn on a tiny enamel badge only) when the occasion demands it. Lads like him, and certainly lads in the proper hoolie firms, tend not to talk about their activities too openly, for obvious legal reasons but also because – very Englishly – it's 'not the done thing'. Those that shout loudest about what they've seen or been caught up in are the outer ring: non-fighters who run into aggro accidentally and don't hang about lest they're called upon to honour the badge.

Liam and Guigsy never even made that last group. Liam didn't go to games as a teenager, although he now gives a very good impression of a City-mad football hooligan; while Guigsy's one and only encounter with aggro took place on January 13, 1990, after he'd attended a rare away game at White Hart Lane. Spurs' deceptively cultured reputation fools many an away-day-tripper. They have handy firms, like most London clubs, and ran City's fans ragged, Guigsy included, all over the Seven Sisters area for a good half-hour. Guigs confessed to Chris, following his experience, that he'd never go away with City again. And as long as Chris knew him, he didn't.

Noel, sadly, is a classic of the outer-ring type. He undoubtedly put in some good mileage with brother Paul ('Bod') during City's Second Division season in 83/4. But one cringes to read his blathering to Hewitt: 'We called ourselves the Young Governors and then it got changed to the Cool Cats . . . we spent two years running up and down the street like those scenes in *Quadrophenia*. It was a good laugh.' First, as almost any United casual, let alone a City boy, would know, the

Governors succeeded the Cool Cats years later. Second, the idea that Noel was a member of any such outfit is somewhat improbable. Indeed, no City boy Chris knew has ever seen Noel actually fighting at football at any time. As for it all being a 'good laugh', it doesn't appear from his brother's book that Noel enjoyed the only serious trouble he ever encountered, at Wembley in '86. There, *real* Young Guv'nor equivalents were in action for the tinpot Full Members' Cup – Chelsea's firms, who caused havoc all day with GBH and knifings a-plenty. The Gallaghers, understandably, shat themselves. Nothing wrong in that, of course – unless you want to boast to your official biographer that you were some sort of main boy.

Chris, by contrast, came face-to-face with unhinged bedlam virtually the first time he stepped outside Manchester. He'd been going to United since 1976, when his dad bought him his own League Match Ticket Book and was told by the club that he was now the youngest LMTB-er in the ground. By 1984, he'd graduated into the Stretford End, on his own. Later, he'd be part of the infamous three or four years of the United Road Paddock's heyday. Burnage Reds – who included Chris and his mates Macca, Ritchie and Stevie – might have been outnumbered by Blues in the area, but they made up for it in man-hours, doing at least 15 aways each season. During the shakier seasons, Chris might have had to come back to face the Blue music in the Milestone pub but he could

always turn around to the likes of Guigsy and say
'What the fuck do you know? If you don't go, you
don't know.' Unanswerable, pre-Sky.

April 1985: Chris is 14, heading for Hillsborough on
the Special train, the first time he's been able to afford
a proper, non-derby away-day. He'd heard there might
be a bit of trouble – unfinished business from the year
Wednesday went down – but he was still amazed to
see the hundreds going for it in the Leppings Lane
End. A mad return was guaranteed by a 1-0 defeat,
title-chasing United's first since January. Chris watched
transfixed as Reds wrecked the Special, chucking seats
out of the window, pulling the com-cord at every stop
so they could fight on platforms. Eventually, the Reds
got their wish: the police invaded the train, only to be
humiliated as Reds charged through them and headed
for a nearby pub, which took a thorough bricking. It
was savage, appalling, dangerous and . . . extremely
exhilarating. Chris was hooked.

That meant accepting a fair share of hidings too
over the seasons. Bricked on every trip to Anfield and
Goodison, bottled and bricked by dozens of Geordies
from the top of the park wall at St James', chased
across East London by mental Hammers – but still he
kept going back. Occasionally, he'd feel the privilege of
being in with the top boys: in '85/6, he ended up on
the service train with a feared Salford firm on the way
to defeat at Sunderland. The police staged one of the
biggest operations seen up there just in order to keep
these hundred lads from the opposition – 'It seemed

there were three pigs to every Red.'

The inevitable occurred later in the eighties: the moment you think you're going to die. Chris got arrested at West Ham, live on TV too, after he took exception to the repeated 'Munich '58' chants from the pen next to his. For giving a few multi-fingered salutes, he was promptly carted off in full view of the pitch for 'inciting a riot'. The game hadn't even kicked off. Placed in a holding cell, he was released at 3.05, finding himself alone outside the ground with the turnstiles closed. Then, the most blood-curdling moment of his life, worse than any approach to Anfield or Goodison: a roar of 'ICF! ICF!', right behind him. He turned to see about 150 of the Inter-City Firm, getting escorted to their *own* ground. To Chris, his tiny enamel badge suddenly felt like it was a dustbin lid. He legged it to the corner, to try and jib in through the away-end turnstiles – but there, loitering with intent, stood a pack of Hammer Under-Fives. One pointed at him, and the others turned to see the quarry like that scene from *Invasion of the Body-Snatchers*. He possibly broke his own school 400-metre record exiting the area. Luckily, he found a perfect hidey-hole in the coach park and listened as the pack roared by. He was back again the following season, of course – but with the badge inside the lapel.

For Chris, the highlights remained the derby matches. In '87, he'd got involved in a riot down Oldham Street as gangs marauded, putting in pub windows and howling with bloodlust. Later, he was amongst those escorted from the Kippax corner to the Platt Lane corner in '89, buzzing as the Reds chanted 'United aggro', knowing that a day of bedlam was guaranteed. It would perhaps entail running up against Burnage mates who were Blues, a bitter-sweet dilemma. When he was 14, he'd engaged in the fringes of the enormous kick-off that followed United's 1985 piss-taking 3-0 Maine Road victory. At one point, a really good mate from school was only yards away, fighting his Blue corner; only an intervention from the police horses prevented them clashing face-to-face. At school, once the 48-hour period of post-derby incommunicado had passed, the boys discussed the hypothetical scenario: what to do if faced by a mate in a football ruck? The consensus was brutal but clear: as Chris concluded, 'if it's Red v Blue, I'd have to do you.' In Manchester, football *matters*.

Had Chris been a few years older, such incidents would have been weekly rather than monthly – casual aggro's high-water mark had been between 1981 and 1985. The year of Heysel, Hillsborough and rioting Millwallians had clearly altered the climate on the terraces, a process which would be accelerated by the arrival of 'Madchester's good vibes'. As an obsessive match-goer, Chris could hardly fail to notice one example of new terrace phenomena at Old Trafford: inflatable skeletons. (United-haters were quick to spread the myth that these were some sort of sick reference to the late Bill Shankly, which was clearly wrong given that Shanks was buried over seven years earlier.) The inflatable craze was eventually picked up by the sloth-like media, who trumpeted a new terrace culture based on pre-Vic Reeves surrealist humour – and fuelled by the new aroma that was crowding out the Bovril fumes: cannabis smoke.

Guigs and his fellow Blues were quick to claim credit for these developments as proof that City fans were in the vanguard of footie street-cred. (Though it's widely alleged that they stole the inflatable/stoned image from some lower division wasters, à la Blue Moon.) Still, as home of many of the city's drug-dealing wide-boys, Maine Road might just have a valid claim there. Not that Chris cared, recognizing that it was a sad situation when a club's pretensions to greatness are based on plastic bananas instead of silver trophies.

Dope at Mancunian football certainly pre-dated Ecstasy at the Haçienda. Scruffy and baggy had already been 'in' at both Old Trafford and Maine Road for a couple of seasons before 1988's Summer of Love: it looked like inflatable clothes were an inevitable corrolary of blow-up fruit and animals. Wildly flapping flares were retrieved from attics, and shaggy hair and voluminous T-shirts became an increasingly common sight around town on a Saturday afternoon. And secreting a few ready-rolled spliffs beat having to smuggle beer into grounds. There were times, look-ing at the Old Trafford goalmouths, when you felt there was more grass in the stands than on the pitch. Although it would be pat to draw a direct causal link between the decline of aggro and the rise of the zine-reading, baggy-bedecked, mellowed-out fan, the atmosphere had certainly changed. However, never imagine that late-eighties Manchester was one huge drug-induced love-in – the infamous terrace battle at the Maine Road derby in '89 was hardly the expected behaviour of stoners, was it? In truth, the period between Hillsborough and the end of the decade was never as easily characterized as the media wanted it to be. If aggro had become less popular, and certainly less fashionable, after 1985, it certainly never declined to the extent that it did during New Football's honeymoon period of 1992-95. Indeed, in some ways it turned out to be a golden era for a small minority in the hardcore firms such as West Ham's Inter-City Firm and Leeds's Service Crew, who saw the part-time hoolies and runners drop away, leaving only the devoted thugs to face similarly committed opposition.

Yet that swinging constituency who had temporarily turned the other cheek to aggro could always be won back at any time, given circumstances such as the derby in '89. As both Kippax and North Stand exploded into violence that afternoon, forcing a delay to the play and inspiring an evening of post-match mayhem in town, it was clear this had not been the work of merely one or two hardcore firms. Those diverted by Madchester's vibes, by the fanzines and inflatables, and by the common cross-club cause against authority and ID cards, could always revert to type.

For Manchester was and is a violent, hard city and

Madchester represented only a truce, not an armistice. Southern students who raced to the city's colleges, expecting to find the Haight-Ashbury of the North, soon discovered the bitter truth as the city's essence reasserted itself at the turn of the decade. What happened to the Haçienda and other clubs, as 'Gunchester' replaced its smiley-faced predecessor in the headlines, was harshly symbolic.

The bristling proletarian aggression which sizzles within Oasis's music and attitude is the only truly Manc thing about them. One of the extraordinary features of the music produced by the Stone Roses and Happy Mondays is the *lack* of urban tension and aggro within – all other classic local bands made music rooted in angst, fear and discord. The Smiths may have been led by a flower-waving, veggie egg-head but so much of their material was inspired by violent lives in a violent city, reflecting both the horror and appeal of aggro. So Morrissey might talk about the shuddering memories of being chased by Rusholme ruffians across Piccadilly Bus Station every Saturday, but he'll spend his nights hanging around boxing halls and use aggressive metaphors about causing injury to those whom he loathes. It's another Manc paradox: this is possibly the friendliest, most welcoming city in Britain, yet probably produces more batterings per square mile than any other. (Bar Glasgow a.k.a. Mad Bastard Central, perhaps.)

The period 1987–90 would be Manchester's interregnum, an occasionally joyous but sometimes uneasy alliance between usually hostile forces. Indie-heads and dance-kids broke off from mutual suspicion to share some cross-fertilized nights and records. Some Blues and Reds turned to fanzines and piss-taking black humour instead of half-bricks. Clubs were allowed to be run by club people while the gangsters held back outside the city centre. Locals and students, united in their enjoyment of the cultural explosion around them, maintained a relationship other than that of burglar/basher and victim. But it was never going to last.

No 'scene' ever endures for more than a year once it's been nationally exposed, once outside corrosive forces have started to eat away at its spirit. The abdication of the leaders, the Roses and Mondays, removed any last hope for survival, as they surrendered to the hedonistic self-indulgence upon which much of Madchester was based anyway. The nineties violence of the kind witnessed at the Maine Road derby in '95, or indeed at the Oasis Maine Road gig in '96, is more typically Mancunian than any legendary blissed-out Haç night in '88 ever was. When the unnatural stimulus of E disappeared, nature's testosterone was still there, ready to come on as sub.

4

Heaven Knows
I'm Miserable Now

The Smiths by Pat Gilbert

It was the summer of 1986. Punk was ten years old. Not quite a faded irrelevance, you'll understand, but no longer something that exerted a direct influence on music, in terms of either people embracing it or rallying against it. Punk was fast becoming just another blast from the past, a turbulent chapter in history that had evolved into a hundred tangled storylines. Times had changed.

For one, the musical centre of gravity had moved north. It was the big industrial cities – Manchester, Liverpool, Leeds – which were now producing the most thrilling pop sounds; reviving a tradition that had started back in the early sixties with the Beatles and the Hollies, but which somehow faltered at some indeterminate point in the seventies. For all the insipid chart fodder, 1986 was arguably the first year that is instantly recognizable as 'modern':

during those 12 months, music finally regained its sense of purpose.

As an instinctive celebration of this fact, and of its growing pre-eminence as a city of culture, Manchester hosted a one-day music festival on July 19 at the enormous G-MEX Centre, converted from the shell of a Victorian railway terminus. The line-up read like an Olympian roll-call of the Manchester good and great – New Order, the Smiths, the Fall, Buzzcocks' Pete Shelley, poet John Cooper Clarke.

It seemed curious that New Order should be headlining over the Smiths. After all, the latter were, at the time, the most fêted band in Britain. They'd only recently unleashed their third and finest album, *The Queen is Dead*, and were set to preview a non-album single called 'Panic', whose incitement to 'burn down the disco' and 'hang the dee-jay' was already earning them radio-bans and (somewhat absurdly) accusations of racism in the press. Yet second on the bill they were – for all it mattered. They took the stage in broad daylight, with a watery sun filtering through the dusty panes of the huge arch roofs, and to an incredible roar from the crowd that sounded like the baying of a thousand sacrificial animals.

Morrissey, wearing white Levi's and a polka-dot blouse, seemed a little anxious to be up there in front of a home crowd; but then the group kicked into 'Bigmouth Strikes Again' and the whole place exploded into a euphoric, dizzying outbreak of unfettered emotion. Live, the Smiths had always offered a release, Morrissey safe in the knowledge that he was more than capable of invoking a quasi-religious fervour from his predominantly male audience. But this was something else. This was the band as a primitive, rock'n'roll engine.

Bassist Andy Rourke's heroin problem had worsened in the early months of 1986; an auxiliary second guitarist, 20-year-old Craig Gannon, had been drafted in. This augmented line-up freed up the group's mercurial lead guitarist and co-songwriter, Johnny Marr, to play in a wilder, less mannered style, the duty of reproducing his intricate fretwork now shared with his understudy.

The result, seen in Manchester, was an incredible metallic wall-of-sound, something akin to an imaginary Phil Spector production for the Velvet Underground or the Byrds. On-stage, the tension was extreme to the point of being frightening. All four musicians stood stock still, the guitarists' hands chopping rabidly at their strings, drummer Mike Joyce pounding his kit like a mechanical hammer. The immobile poses, the lazy, nonchalant stares, the sheer confidence that comes with the knowledge that you're the most influential band of your era – there was something about the Smiths that foreshadowed Oasis's 'triumphs' at Maine Road a decade alter. Only Morrissey showed signs of animation, striking his trademark hand-on-hip poses and looking forlornly towards the iron beams in the roof.

The Smiths were creatures of light and shade, and after a suite of melancholic numbers, including the astonishingly beautiful 'There Is A Light That Never Goes Out' and aching 'Cemetery Gates', Joyce's thunderous tom-toms led the group into 'The Queen Is Dead'. Morrissey was in his element, his nimble, gyrating frame grabbing a placard bearing the song's title, which he then held high above his ample quiff in some bizarre but totally congruous theatrical gesture that said everything about his band's exquisite grasp of the painfully ironic and the deadly serious. Behind him, Marr, Gannon, Rourke and Joyce cooked up a swirling, chopping, psychedelic barrage of full-on noise, reaching a crescendo that slowly died away into cascading ripples of wah-wah guitar and a clunky, trebly bass mantra.

There are times in your life when music can penetrate your whole soul, and make the chaos of life make sense: that was one of them. Within a year of their G-MEX performance, though, the Smiths had split. In their five years together, they'd released four studio albums, two rarities compilations and a live LP – it was enough to secure their reputation as the most important British group of the 1980s.

John Peel once said of the Smiths that they were one of the few bands in rock history that sounded as if 'they'd sprung full arm'd from the ground'. Though you could detect certain influences (the Byrds' jangly guitar sounds is one that springs to mind), he pointed out, they didn't at any point sound like anyone else. They were, it seemed, almost wholly original, at a time when the general consensus was that rock music had run out of ideas. What the Smiths sounded like was very much down to Johnny Marr, the group's musical director and still widely regarded as one of the greatest guitarists of his generation, if such things can be measured. Yet what the Smiths meant was largely a reflection of Morrissey's unique and fascinating perspective on a world he wanted to both conquer and keep at arm's length.

Born in Manchester in 1959, Steven Patrick Morrissey had two early influences that shaped his life (three, if you count his parents' separation in his teens, though Johnny Rogan's Smiths biography, *The Severed Alliance*, suggests that it wasn't quite as traumatic an experience for the singer as he has made out). These defining elements were the Moors Murders and his discovery of sixties pop music. Both occurred around the same time, in 1965, and both affected him in very different ways.

The murders – of five children by Ian Brady and Myra Hindley – alerted Morrissey to a macabre adult world of sex, torture, killing, betrayal, and also to the social taboos associated with talking about such incidents. Meanwhile, the records by the likes of Marianne Faithfull, Cilla Black, Sandie Shaw and Dusty Springfield stirred a passion in him for classic melodies, and no doubt also a dislocated yearning for these far-off objects of desire.

Intelligent, sensitive, athletic, Morrissey had none of the disabilities that you'd expect from a nascent symbol of worship for insecure adolescent males. The only attribute that bothered him was the shyness he would sing about in 'How Soon Is Now?' He fared averagely at school, but his academic studies were overshadowed by his love of music. By the mid-seventies he was a regular correspondent to the letters pages of the music weeklies, and even wrote a short book on his glam-punk heroes, The New York Dolls. A couple of years later, he was reviewing gigs and even fronting his own band, the Nosebleeds, also including Billy Duffy (later of the Cult).

Morrissey was, though, a definite misfit – bashful, aloof,

painfully awkward in the presence of women he didn't know. Manchester journalist Paul Morley told the writer Nick Kent: 'In the Joy Division days, when everybody was going round carrying a copy of Nietzsche, you'd see Morrissey at a bus stop looking hopeless and reading Sven Hassel.' One suspects Morley was exaggerating, but there was always a sense in Manchester that this young, introspective aesthete from Stretford was an eternal outsider.

Morrissey was living an ascetic bedsit life by the time he teamed up with Johnny Marr in May 1982. He was spending his days reading, letter-writing and honing his lyrics – almost exclusively at the expense of the taxpayer. The Smiths were keen to create their own mythology, and many tales have been told about the fateful meeting between the two men. According to Morrissey, Marr turned up unannounced and left sticky chocolate fingerprints on his window-sill; the guitarist claims he went round and knocked on this stranger's door because that was how it happened with Leiber and Stoller.

They were in fact, introduced by a mutual friend – not half so interesting a tale, but the result was ultimately the same. Morrissey and Marr began collaborating on songs like 'Suffer Little Children' (a fragile, quite beautiful ballad about the Moors victims) and the dour, enrapturing 'Reel Around The Fountain'. They became inseparable.

Johnny Marr was just 18 at the time, Morrissey 22. Born Johnny Maher, the guitarist became an accomplished musician when he was still at school, learning his craft from playing Rory Gallagher, Rolling Stones and Crosby, Stills, Nash & Young songs with a school band called White Dice. As he would later point out, Marr was too young to have engaged with punk, and instead his music tapped into the classic seventies singer-songwriter tradition that the new wave had set out to destroy. He never claimed to be a lyricist; and now he'd found his ideal collaborator.

So it was that the Smiths were born, in the early summer of 1982, Johnny having drafted in his old schoolfriend and White Dice bassist, Andy Rourke, and a local drummer, Mike Joyce. From the beginning, it was clear that the group were unique. Morrissey and Marr shared the same artistic vision, agreeing that the group ought to be peculiarly Mancunian and distinct from anything that had gone before. The name they chose was a celebration of a certain kind of humdrum 'Northernness'.

In recent years, Morrissey had become enamoured with the spate of late-fifties films and books which had given a bittersweet account of contemporary life in the Midlands and the North. In time, he would cite *Billy Liar*, *Saturday Night & Sunday Morning*, *Room at the Top* and *A Taste of Honey* as among his favourite works. Romantic, witty, sardonic, self-deprecating, their atmosphere was to permeate his lyrics, as much as his love of rockabilly and sixties 'girl groups' was later to quietly influence the direction of The Smiths' sound. His abiding muse, though, was Oscar Wilde, whose ability to toss off an aphorism at the drop of a cravat was quickly mastered by Morrissey in the hundreds of interviews he was about to give.

Things happened quickly for the group. In 1983, a London gig led to the release of a single on Rough Trade, 'Hand in Glove', followed later that year by their first *bona fide* hit, 'This Charming Man'. The press didn't know quite what to make of this Mancunian quartet, whose frontman styled himself on James Dean and performed on stage with a spray of daffodils stuffed into his back pocket. Yet there was a nagging realization that they might be the greatest thing to happen in music since punk.

When *NME* cartoonist Ray Lowry lampooned the band for being 'wimps', he was unwittingly touching on an area in which the Smiths were sending confusing signals: sexual politics. The truth was that Morrissey was about to revolutionize attitudes towards male sexuality, just as Madonna was for women on a more global scale. 'Hand in Glove' had been an us-against-the-world love song for the denizens of bedsit land but it was patently clear to anyone who listened carefully that 'This Charming Man' was loaded with homo-erotic imagery, as well as the first in a long line of references to impotence.

Until this point, rock songs had invariably fallen into three categories: love songs, protest songs and story-telling songs. Never had anyone written so graphically about the self-perceived physical and emotional inadequacies of post-pubescent males. Pop music has been a history of the unrequited lover, but no one had ever come out and said that the other sex were mildly distasteful.

When the Smiths' self-titled debut album emerged in 1984, it amounted to the ultimate statement of bewildered adolescence, as refracted through Morrissey's unnervingly downbeat world view and Johnny Marr's eloquent, jazz-inspired chord progressions. It wasn't an easy album to warm to: the delicacy of 'Suffer Little Children' was never going to fully atone for the wilful abrasion of 'Miserable Lie', not would the poetry of 'Reel Around the Fountain' (with its lines lifted from *A Taste of Honey*) ever compensate for the sardonic misogyny of 'Pretty Girls Make Graves'.

Yet for all its shortcomings, *The Smiths* was an astonishing record. Within months of its release, Morrissey became the cover-star of almost every magazine on the news-stand. At the same time, when the secret about the Smiths' brilliance out of the bag, the weeklies shifted their attentions to Marr, recognizing the whiff of genius in his arrangements. Back then, Marr wore his hair in a Byrdsian basin-cut, dripped with love-beads and applied eye-liner. However, one couldn't help but detect that he was, beyond the foppish front, the archetypal guitar-slinger, fag dangling from pursed lips, a couple of Keith Richard shapes among his repertoire of stage poses.

For a year, the Smiths were in danger of over-exposing themselves, and on singles like 'Heaven Knows I'm Miserable Now' came perilously close to self-parody. But in 1985 they returned with 'How Soon Is Now?', possibly one of the most innovative rock records of all time. For the immense shimmering guitar sound, Marr linked together a stack of Roland amps and set their vibrators slightly out of phase with one another, so the bank of speakers throbbed on their own. Whining shards of guitar were overdubbed, while Morrissey moaned softly abut the pain of acute shyness.

The Smiths were getting tougher and tighter – though Morrissey remained aloof from the other band members, forsaking their on-tour drinking sessions for the tranquility of an empty hotel room and a good book. He personally checked tour accounts and royalty statements, keeping an iron grip on the band's finances that would lead to litigation with a disgruntled Rourke and Joyce after the band's split. 'I'm not a rock'n'roll character,' he told *Time Out*, 'I despise cigarettes, I'm celibate and I live a very serene lifestyle.' Later, it would emerge just how polarized Morrissey and the other members' lifestyles were becoming.

A radio sessions and rarities compilation, *Hatful of Hollow*, was followed in February 1985 by the release of a second studio album, *Meat is Murder*. Its title-track wheezed with the cruel sounds of abattoir stun guns against a plaintive waltzing beat. Morrissey and Marr were, of course, vegetarians, and coerced Rourke and Joyce to forgo their carnivorous eating habits. (Playing the song on tour a few months later, Morrissey was hit by a string of sausages engraved with the legend 'meat is murder'. The singer put the incident down to 'misguided affection'.) Elsewhere, the album showed a remarkable progression towards a sophisticated rock sound. 'Barbarism Begins At Home' was a particularly dramatic landmark, adding an angular funk dimension to their music, while 'Headmaster Ritual' and the skiffle-inspired 'Rusholme Ruffians' returned to the classic Morrissey territory of adolescent angst.

Meat is Murder consolidated the Smiths' reputation as the finest guitar group in Britain. There was a sense that the album was a culturally pivotal moment, and not just for its dietary statements. The Smiths were changing people's perceptions about maleness: by their very existence, they seemed to be promoting a culture in which young men could be both sensitive *and* masculine. Morrissey was quickly establishing himself as an agony aunt for the sexually uncertain; he understood the hurt of rejection. Marr, conversely, was the impish boy-about-town – happily married to his longtime girlfriend by this time, but increasingly adopting the kind of post-rock swagger that Ian Brown, John Squire and Liam Gallagher would later claim as their own. Between the pair of them, they pretty much had it all worked out.

That summer, the group set off to conquer America, with a considerable degree of success. But the grind of the Hotel Inn circuit inevitably brought with it 'touring psychosis'. Marr demanded that each rider should include tuna sandwiches (no butter), plus a bottle of Jack Daniels – if they didn't, it would result in hell for the tour manager. Meanwhile, Rourke was enduring his own flames of torment, thanks to his inexorable descent into heroin addiction. Joyce drank himself stupid, while Morrissey simply kept his distance from the carnage. He didn't approve.

Ironically, the Smiths were poised for their greatest artistic moment. The galloping, sub-rockabilly rhythm of 'Big Mouth Strikes Again' preceded the release in May 1986 of the group's triumphant third outing, The Queen is Dead. By this time, Rourke's drug problem had got out of hand. He'd already been sacked, replaced by ex-Aztec Camera and Bluebells guitarist Craig Gannon, and then reinstated when he resolved to keep well away from the stuff. Gannon was kept on, shifting to rhythm guitar. Morrissey claimed ignorance about his band member's habit – maybe it was as unthinkable to him as it was to his fans that a Smith could have something so horrifically clichéd as a junk problem.

The depth and variety of the album (rockabilly, metallic white-outs, wistful ballads, music hall) was breathtaking, and ensured ecstatic reviews and a No. 2 chart placing. Meanwhile, the controversy that surrounded 'Panic' (NME journalist Paolo

Hewitt decided the phrase 'Burn down the disco' was a slur on black music; 'Hang the dee-jay' understandably rubbed the daytime jocks up the wrong way) only served to heighten the group's image as a cerebral rebels. In concert, the band cocked a snook at their detractors by mutating into a magnificent metal monster, assured of their place in the history books.

Towards the end of the year, after further touring, Gannon was sacked for either 'being miserable', not contributing enough musical ideas (though he later successfully sued for royalties from 'Ask'), or being 'completely unreliable' – take your pick. By this time, the special something that once radiated from the Smiths' every pore was fast evaporating. Another odds'n'sods compilation, *The World Won't Listen*, anthologized Gannon's tenure, but behind the scenes, management problems, drugs, drink and egos were tearing the original four-piece apart.

Though the sessions for their next album, *Strangeways Here We Come*, resulted in some of the most accomplished material of their career ('Girlfriend In A coma', 'Unhappy Birthday' and the curiously prophetic 'A Vulgar Picture'), the group had split up by the time the record came out in September 1987. The final straw had been Morrissey's non-appearance at a video shoot (he didn't believe in them) and his insistence that the group return to the studio to record some B-sides when Marr pressed for a much-needed break.

But it went deeper than that. The very thing that made the Smiths a monumental rock act was the thing that prised them apart. They were four highly talented and unique individuals, whose artistic vision burned with the kind of blow-torch intensity that was unlikely to last for long. And as with all great bands, history has shown that the Smiths – Morrissey, Marr, Rourke and Joyce – were always greater than the sum of their parts. Oh Manchester, so much to answer for ...

Part Two

5

Reel Around the Fountain

The summer of 1987: Manchester doesn't know it
yet, but it's only months away from the most sud-
den cultural transformation any city's ever undergone. The Fulcrum of Miserabilism to the Epicentre of
Ecstasy in a few pharmacological steps. One apparent
necessity for such a revolution – the Smiths would
have to die, and they duly obliged in August. That
left New Order dominant, the only meaningful musical presence in the city. 'STATE OF THE NATION',
painted large across 25 feet of West Point wall, testified to their status locally. At 16, Chris and Guigsy,
like many in the area, were in thrall to New Order
– and to Joy Division as well. The legend of Ian
Curtis had arguably made them more appreciated by
the mid-eighties than they were in their late seventies heyday, the student jibes forgotten as the band's
emotional force resonated across desolate suburbia.
Only the Smiths had competed for a place in the
boys' affections.

They'd been a little late getting into Morrissey and Marr – incidentally always worshipping the latter more: Levenshulme lads had beaten Burnage to the Smiths' altar and little Marr clones were a frequent sight down Manor Road. As the two became slaves to their record players during upper school, they grew even closer as mates, leading each other into new musical discoveries and beginning to share as yet shapeless dreams about Tonight as a Rock 'n' Roll Star.

Virtually every Saturday night for years, Guigs and Chris would crash at each other's places after a night out; the two would play their latest acquisitions, talk earnestly about lyrics and songs and compare their evolving beliefs. (And Chris began to learn more about the black areas of Guigsy's soul, the depressive and even suicidal sensibilities which he felt as a teenager to which Curtis's lyrics spoke directly.) Like Liam down the road, they were at the age now where one contemporary new band was all that they needed as a catalyst for their subconscious ambitions to surface. Joy Division, the Smiths and New Order were all, in one sense, before the lads' time: all three needed to be in at the start of something, to be able to subsume themselves into a band that was *theirs*. The calling card was actually already out there: Revolver Records had released a low-key single called 'Sally Cinnamon' two months before. Within nine months, Liam, Chris and Guigsy would all have discovered its inspirational auteurs – the Stone Roses.

Not that music had replaced everything in their lives. Football remained a mainstay, though their emphasis differed. Chris had grown up quickly, abandoning his United number five shirt fantasies and settling on being a home-and-away United Road boy, a historic status now prized by those who were there. (If you, like him, were a Red at Newcastle on Boxing Day 1987, you're one of the elite.) Guigsy, however, now tells Hewitt, and anyone else who'll listen, that he 'coulda been a contender', citing supposed trials at Oldham, Crewe and Stockport. Chris is amazed at such claims. Never in all their years as mates did Guigsy mention such a possibility. A sniff of any such opportunity and he'd have been straight round to Chris's to gloat and preen. Guigsy was a decent player, able to hold the ball well and a fair passer, but when he tried out for the school first team, he didn't even make the bench. Clearly, George Best hadn't fully completed Guigsy's footballing education.

No, it wasn't Guigsy's sharp moves on the field that gave him kudos, but his sharp threads. He was always the most comfortably-off in the circle, at least until Bonehead's brother hit it big in the record engineer game. Chris knew that Guigsy wanted for nothing at home from a mother who, having lost her husband, worshipped her son. Chris did his best to keep up but was quietly relieved when the onset of scruffy baggy brought down his own clothing bills. Certainly, until '88, the two wore classic casual, with the odd touch of

Quadrophenia chic. The Phil Daniels film was rarely out of the VCR; only when *Rumblefish* was demanded by Guigsy who, like Eric Cantona, had an unaccountable Mickey Rourke fixation.

Mod influence was quite common around Burnage. The Gallaghers' fat and much-ridiculed older brother was always known as 'Bod the Mod'; Noel had a penchant for scooterism, revived in the nineties once Weller had made such affectations safe again; and Guigsy owned a scooter at 15, although he never appeared to do very much with it, bar one organized scooter club outing. The scene and philosophy suited Guigs, always the most buttoned-down of the lads. That attitude was clearly visible in his ambivalence towards 'hippyish' pot, which Chris was gladly dabbling in wherever possible from an early age; Chris never saw Guigsy on the draw until he was at least 16. When scruffy arrived, along with a loosening of arses all round, Guigs kept it tight, sticking to the casual classics, keeping himself smart and lucid. Once again, Guigs had stepped back a touch, watching from the wings as Manchester went 1967 and off its collective face.

In the rush to credit E for Madchester, too many have forgotten weed's importance. Long before anyone had even heard of Ibiza, or MDMA, weed's image had been completely refurbished. Throughout the eighties, it became universally acceptable for working-class lads to smoke what was once seen as the bourgeois balm. After years of having to rely on speed and glue, this was a relief. Draw opened the doors of Manchester's mind to the drugs and events that followed in the late-eighties. In that narrow respect, the anti-drugs bigots are right to say that pot leads on to more serious (ab)uses. An apt measure of weed's status: next to West Point's 'State of the Nation' graffito soon appeared an enormous painted representation of a cannabis plant. We were already sorted for leaves and Rizz.

Employment opportunities in eighties Manchester did not exactly amount to a glittering range of riches and fulfilment. The celebrated village industry in Manchester, revolving around the music and fashion businesses, certainly existed before Madchester gave it a whole new horizon. But it was hardly of sufficient size to embrace the thousands of lads like Chris who left the sink schools without qualifications at 16. The devastation caused by Thatcherism to the manufacturing base never was, and never will be, compensated for by growth in the service sectors.

Nevertheless, most Mancunians tend not to use that as an excuse for dole-slacking. The residual influences of what made Manchester great – free trade, the work ethic, provincial pride and an aversion to self-pitying sentimentality – still push Mancunians to get on their bikes, however bleak the outlook. Chris may not have dreamt of working in a Longsight factory 50 weeks a year but he was never going to turn it down once he found the job. Guigsy stacked shelves in Gateway, did a stint at Barclays Bank and then landed a cushy number at BT. Even the Gallaghers worked more often than not, despite their Scouse-scally affectations.

When dole-chic was trendy during the last years of Majorism, Liam would often boast about his supplementary benefit bravura, of how he used to tell various stuffed shirts where to insert their job offers. However, the official Oasis record speaks of several Liam engagements, and they're just the ones he'll admit. Chris remembers that he used to get the 50 bus into town with him every morning – Liam, the regular little commuter? He was doing something on the doors of an establishment in town, but he never wanted to elaborate upon it. The fact remains that for most of his post-school years, Liam was more likely to be getting his nose to the grindstone than not.

It's bizarre and unusual that he should want to pretend otherwise. Manchester has a proper social solidarity that Liverpool lacks. Here, if you're genuinely out of work, the community does not begrudge you the assistance it finances; but if you're skiving, you're robbing your neighbours, some of whom will give a quiet cheer if the DSS catch you. Similarly, the Gallaghers have waxed lyrical about their supposed burglaries, at least until Inspector Knacker pricked up his piggy ears. As investigations have made clear, there was nothing to this: so why make the boast? Burglars and scroungers may be heroic figures in Anfield, but not in Burnage. Indeed, the result of this reckless posturing is that many Mancunians – especially of the Red kind – now sneer that the Gallaghers are not proper Mancunians at all, but pseudo-Scousers. Perhaps it's all a function of the strange interaction between Oasis and their home city, whereby the Gallaghers often seem to be both embracing and rejecting their roots simultaneously.

At least back then, pre-fame, Liam sounded more like one of the lads. When Mark Shenton secured Liam's first ever job for him at a printers, Parfitt's, the foreman gave the brooding Gallagher his work detail – menial drudgery of the most demeaning kind. An appalled Liam turned round and snarled: 'That's bang out of order. What do you think I am? I'm telling ya, in three years time I'll be so famous you'll be kissing me arse – kissing me arse and lovin' it.' But he still did the work. That combination of defiance and graft, done with a swagger, is much more Manc attitude.

For Chris, work meant money; money meant beer, gigs and football. And for Guigsy you substitute designer clobber for football. After a summer of having the piss taken after City's second relegation of the eighties, Guigs was even less inclined to initiate the home-and-away compulsiveness of Chris. Not that Chris was seeing the best, as United bored and blundered their way through the early Ferguson years. But he was hooked in a way Guigsy never was. Chris was already a veteran of battles at Anfield, St James' and Upton Park; even at 18, Guigsy still hadn't seen City away from Maine Road. For Guigs and Noel, a politically correct professed devotion to City has proved useful in a United-hating world, but its foundation is shakier than Maine Road's finances.

The area's pubs awaited. The boys were still two years underage but had beer tokens a-plenty, which is the only figure most publicans are concerned with. The Packhorse in Levenshulme's Stockport Road was the local lads' pub of choice: no bloody fruit in your lager and punch-ups guaranteed. Bonehead was a regular there, ready with the laddish bonhomie; Noel would sometimes be lurking in the shadows, working on the Masterplan. Six pints there, then off to see the Macc Lads, maybe the odd Groltsch bottling and a bit of a skirmish afterwards – that was a good night out, circa early 1988. Special occasions came courtesy of the odd New Order or ACR gig, sometimes with a side-order of Happy Mondays, who were still trying to push the *Squirrel and G-Man* album. The more perspicacious had already seen the symbolic changeover: a month after The Smiths' last LP, *Strangeways Here We Come*, the Mondays had released the single '24 Hour Party People', a cognoscenti favourite. A change in mood and times, but the Mondays were still a curiosity rather than the inevitable future.

Chris looks back fondly on the Packhorse days now. The music was bang off, the kick-offs regular, the banter top. He even met his missus there, his success being greeted with disbelief by Guigsy who had solemnly predicted 'You'll never pull there in a million years'. Uncomplicated times, when no one really knew where they were heading in life but were determined to make the most of it in the meantime. All that changed forever on the night of May 29, 1988 when the Stone Roses rode into town to conquer the International 2 venue. The Gallaghers, and several other Burnage lads, witnessed a Messianic performance, and Liam emerged with a mission for life. Word got around town: after three years of seemingly aimless fannying about, the Roses were the real thing at last. Within a year, they would have produced the greatest album of the Eighties – and in turn inspired the creation of the biggest band of the nineties.

Chris had no idea how Liam had been affected – the last time he'd noticed anything about Liam's musical tastes was hearing him banging on about electro and hip-hop, which meant little to most Burnage lads. Where did he think we were, the Bronx? You can still raise a smile from those who witnessed it by mentioning Liam's ridiculous break-dancing and head-spinning outside KwikSave. But he knew Noel had caught the Roses vibe.

Around Christmas '88, Guigsy pointed out Noel in the Packhorse – he hadn't been in for a while – and told Chris that Noel had been auditioning for the Inspiral Carpets vocalist vacancy. He'd failed but had been offered a roadie's job; he was on the rock and roll ladder. Someone who'd overheard them chipped in that Noel was a bit of a songwriter too – he'd been doing a few bits and pieces on tape and wanted to be in a band. 'Don't we all?' thought Chris. But he was impressed that someone from their circle had broken through, in however modest a fashion. At least he'd be out touring, not stuck in a factory.

The carefree Packhorse days were numbered, as they are for any pub whose underage clientele likes to wreck the joint from time to time. A police raid scattered the lads across the area, and the 'horse put gorillas on the door (one of whom was later battered by a disillusioned ex-regular). Chris's boys eventually found refuge at the Milestone on Burnage Lane. At least it'd be easier to stagger home from there, as Chris lived only yards away. Bonehead's posse came with them – but they were all appalled by the state of the music and general clientele there.

Throughout 1989, as Madchester exploded, the same scene unfolded at the Milestone as in hundreds of out-posts across the city. For what happened in Manchester then was not confined to the well-known clubs and venues within the city's central square mile, the places that attracted the beau monde and later the tourists. This wasn't just some trendy metropolitan fad but a cultural phenomenon, barging its way into every point of social gathering across the region. Even before the Roses debut album was released, the Milestone and its equivalents were simply taken over by the Madchester spirit, by forcible punter-power. Hordes of lads in baggy T-shirts crowded out any non-believers, turning normal pub nights into events. Crap DJ and music? Then do-it-yourself. Guigsy's superb record collection got transported bit by bit into the Milestone to provide a proper Manchester soundtrack. As a new Milestone regular remarked during a year of good vibes and getting high, 'If we can't afford to go to the Haç every night, then we'll have to bring a bit of the Haç into here.'

Carried along by the spirit of liberation Madchester induced – which taught by example that you could do this music lark too – Chris began getting up on the small stage to do a turn or two, belting out 'True Faith' during his 18th bash and 'Blue Monday' for Guigsy's at his request. Secretly, Chris was chuffed by the response: instead of the usual piss-taking such behaviour generally guarantees, the lads seemed quietly impressed, egging him on to 'go into one' and put on a performance. He'd throw in a few Curtis moves, mess about a bit, play off the lads' raucous reactions; he was loving it. If it wasn't yet a conscious, concrete ambition, then he'd at least set out on the path to be a singer. After all, if you can do it for your mates, doing it for punters is a piece of piss.

6

Golden Lights

For Chris, 1989 was the *annus mirabilis* – a never-ending succession of delights tumbling down upon him. Personally, he'd found his soul-mate, and by August she was in the club; musically, *The Stone Roses*, *Technique* and *Bummed* dominated the boys' lives, supported by classic singles such as 'Joe', 'Made of Stone' and 'W. F. L.'. And even United appeared to be doing the business at last. Chris vividly remembers the opening day of the 89/90 football season. He was in United Road, taking the missus to her first game. It had been a glorious summer, soundtracked by the Roses album and climaxing at their legendary Blackpool gig; now Michael Knighton had turned up at Old Trafford, promising millions and a championship future. That August afternoon, as United destroyed Title-holders Arsenal 4-1 in brilliant sunshine, was a peak of sorts. Madchester was exploding yet remained largely a local secret; United were back, and even sad City had managed promotion; Neil

Webb and Ian Brown were gods not fallen idols;
the Inspirals were our favourite pop puppies, not
jokes; drugged-out bliss was in everyone's eyes . . .
simply, Manchester felt like the centre of the universe instead of a provincial outpost of drudgery.

Every month brought a new and seemingly epochal
event. In July the legendary Roses' Blackpool gig.
October: half of Burnage decamped en masse to Paris
for a delirious Roses/La's gig where Guigsy and Tony
French cheered as 'Hodge' leapt skywards to catch
Reni's drumsticks. November: Manchester roared as
the Roses lambasted a hapless Tracey McLeod on *The
Late Show* – 'Amateurs, amateurs!' was catchphrase
of the week, pure Manc attitude. November 18: the
greatest Roses event yet, as hundreds of Reds, fresh
from victory at Kenilworth Road, joined the bedlam at the Alexandra Palace. And proudest of all?
Top of the Pops on 30 November, as the Roses and
Mondays brought Madchester to the nation's kids.

Chris recalls the empty streets as every lad stayed
home, glued to the screen, VCRs running by the thousand. Now that *TOTP* has been so grotesquely devalued, this might seem all rather quaint. But at the time,
it felt like the barricades had been stormed: this was
now going big-time big-style. Manchester was showing
the rest of the country how utterly clueless they were
in comparison, stuck in their indie or chart dance ruts,
while it was inventing this extraordinary concoction,
delivered with attitude and style. December's results
appeared inevitable to us: 'Fools Gold' into the Top

Ten, with the 'Rave On' EP on its tail. Anyone with taste or understanding in the London media immediately purchased a Manchester A–Z and headed north. 'It's not where you're coming from, it's where you're at' ran the famous Brownism – and an 061 phone code marked where you had to be.

'061 – good name for a band,' thought Chris. Watching *Top of the Pops* had convinced him that he now had to do something; consuming was no longer enough. If there is one overwhelming argument to support the contention that pop should be led by the young and radical, it is this: no one can inspire the consumer to become the creator quite like one of their own. Seeing a scally from Little Hulton who can barely sing becoming a star teaches every other downtrodden lad with aspirations that he too can do it. This is the real Circle of Pop Life, not the arid transmission of musical values through record-collection rock. Most who try fail, of course – Chris never dreamt that he'd come so agonizingly close to success.

He'd already had an abortive attempt at getting involved even before the *TOTP* watershed moment. An advert had caught his eye in a local paper: 'Singer Wanted For Indie-Pop Band'. Chris mooched round to the guy's house, who gave him a tape of songs already written and demo'd to learn. 'Aren't you from Burnage?' he asked Chris, ''Cos the bloke who used to write with me's from there. That's some of his songs on there, actually. Noel Gallagher was the guy's name – something with the Inspirals now, I think.' But the liaison came to nothing. Chris thought the tape a bit shit and never phoned the guy back.

Noel's stuff in particular seemed aimless and meaningless; still, he was only a roadie wasn't he? He chucked the tape in a cupboard and decided he'd do his own thing instead. The intriguing opportunity to form a Manchester band in 1989 singing Noel Gallagher songs was lost. Never mind: timing is everything in pop and had any band come out with something as retro-trad as 'Shakermaker' in the revolutionary atmosphere of 1989, it would have been ignored anyway.

Through the winter of 89/90, Chris began to formulate his plans. Two fundamentals mattered to him above all. One was that he should try to express himself lyrically, so that he'd never fall into the sad trap of being a vocalist singing someone else's words. Music wasn't a joke or an act to him – he wanted whatever he did to matter. The men he looked up to, Curtis, Brown and even Morrissey, carried emotional weight because they had written what they sang. You could believe in them as individual artists as well as in the groups to which they belonged. Much as he liked the Who, another gift of Guigsy's good taste, he could never take Roger Daltrey seriously even at the height of his pop-art chic – second-hand delivery didn't ring true.

Two, he knew he had to draw from his background: he was Mancunian, born and bred. He'd sung that a thousand times in the United Road Paddock and understood why it felt so powerful. He had a sense of place and belonging which he knew could give grounding to whatever he wrote or sang. He wasn't ashamed to boast of being an English patriot and a Mancunian – this was an identity he embraced. Not for him the ambivalence of the Gallaghers towards their roots; nor, for that matter, Ian Brown's disavowal of Mancunian separatism. Before he'd written a word, he knew any music he was involved in had to be based on Mancunian individual experience, not Everyman generality. Choosing the working title '061' for his project made that clear from the start.

By the end of March 1990, Chris was ready to sound out the boys. This was not a step to take lightly, for poncing around your local with big talk about pop stardom tended to be route one to piss-take frenzy, especially if you crashed and burnt without ever playing a note. But day upon day slaving in a factory had at least given Chris time to think. He'd sit at the workdesk, turning phrases over in his mind, ruminating on song subjects, working out verse patterns – he'd already completed two full songs of a standard good enough to dare showing the other lads. Anyone who's ever committed themselves emotionally and mentally to the mere idea of starting a band knows how exciting these first steps are: how easy it is to lie awake at night thinking of gigs, record covers, song credits, what a buzz it can be to write a line knowing that the day might come when thousands are singing it back to you. Chris was no different: whatever the excitement engendered in him by the prospect of that weekend's Mondays gig at the G-MEX, it was matched by the secret thrill of the artist stirring within.

April 16, 1990: a scorching Bank Holiday Monday in the Milestone is as good a date as any to mark the birth of Oasis. The lads had secured an afternoon lock-in and the air was thick with beer fumes, Strangeways riot gossip and planning for United at Wembley. Chris had carefully planned to add to the agenda. He'd already sounded out old West Pointer Pat Moran about Bonehead. He'd remembered that Bonehead had some kind of musical history – what was that group's terrible name? Pleasure in Pain? – and knew he wasn't yet hooked up with anyone else. He'd only just returned from a six-month jaunt around Europe, before coming back to set up a plastering and decorating business. Still, it was a slightly daunting prospect. Bonehead was a proper head, much older and world-weary. Sure, he'd been a West Pointer but he was always someone to let on to with respect rather than presume upon as an equal. Chris coughed and looked him straight in the eye: 'Bonehead: I'm forming a band. I'm gonna do the singing and the lyrics and I've heard you can play guitar. So d'you fancy it?' No smarm, right to the point. Bonehead paused for a half-second, broke into his trademark grin and replied, 'Mad for it. In fact, I'll do anything except sing or write lyrics. Come round tomorrow and we'll talk.' Easier than he'd dreamed.

Lurking in Bonehead's shadow stood Guigsy, open-mouthed. His mate, with whom he'd bullshitted for years about bands and dreams and stardom, had actually got off his arse and done something about it. Had he not been there to witness the offer to Bonehead, it's unlikely Guigsy would ever have become involved in the band at all. Certainly Chris had never thought of including Guigs – after all, what could he do in a band? Being the singer's best mate was scarcely qualification.

Guigs, however, immediately saw the sliver of an opening, calculated the position, and dived in within five seconds. It was surely the best and luckiest question he ever asked: 'Chris, can I join as well?' Now there's your actual 64 million dollar question for you.

'Guigs, you can't play fuck all mate. What the fuck are you gonna do in a band?' Chris demanded.

'I'll do anything, Chris. Anything.' A tone of desperation was creeping in. 'I'll learn somethin' easy, like the bass. Look, I'll play the fuckin' maracas if necessary.'

A vision of Guigsy as Oasis's Bez lurches horribly into mind.

'I'll have to ask Bonehead tomorrow; that's the best I can do,' reasoned Chris. The group was five seconds old and already he's got his first political crisis. But he knew he couldn't let his best mate down. He would have to argue Guigsy's corner for him with Bonehead, even if it made him look like a complete amateur. ('Can me mate play out too, please mister?')

Within 24 hours, Chris knew he'd made a bang-on

choice with Bonehead. It wasn't merely that Bonehead was buzzing about starting a new band as much as Chris was, or that the array of musical instruments scattered across his room marked him out as a proper music head. It was the sense of generosity and spirit of adventure about him that appealed most of all. Around his room were plastered scores of postcards, mementos of trips he'd made or which his mates had told him about – he was insatiably curious about the world, a true traveller. He talked about the many bands and outfits he'd been in and out of, about the wildly differing styles and fashions he'd sampled, even about his Perry Boy beginnings – he was quite obviously up for anything new. When Chris tentatively proferred his first lyrics, he was instantly positive, boosting Chris's self-esteem. And when Chris finally raised the Guigsy problem, Bonehead just grinned and replied, 'No problem – I'll teach him bass.'

So they had a singer, guitarist and a sort of bassist – but, like virtually every new band ever formed, they'd have to go out and find a drummer. As John Lennon used to say, pre-Best, 'a drummer makes a *group* – otherwise you're just three lads dicking about with guitars'. For the time being, Bonehead's drum machine would have to do. The massive Echo and the Bunnymen poster on his wall already suggested Bonehead wouldn't see this as too much of a hindrance for now and when Chris heard the machine rap out a perfect 'Blue Monday' pattern, he too was convinced.

Next day, Chris told Guigs the good news that he was

in. 'Top one!' Guigs yelped. 'We're gonna be pop stars!' Pleasing positivity – but then, every August he used to declare City would win a trophy. Nevertheless, despite not being able to play a note, Guigsy did the group a sterling first service by declaring that they could rehearse in his front room. Whatever Guigsy wanted, mother would allow, apparently. She'd obviously not heard about Bonehead's love of distortion.

Bonehead had another inanimate godsend available to join the band – the notorious Bonemobile. A battered blue American-style pick-up truck, its decrepitude was legendary. You had to start it with a complicated screwdriver manoeuvre, drive it with the all-senses flair of a fighter pilot, then attempt to slow the bugger down by repeatedly jumping on its brakes at least a minute before you wanted to stop. It just about sufficed to cart the amps and instruments down to Guigsy's house every day, where mother had the tea and digestives waiting and Guigsy hid his fags. Rock'n'roll life, Burnage-style.

For six weeks, the lads laboured together, discovering what each of their imaginations could do. Bonehead's patience was exemplary as he guided Guigsy's novice fingers around his bass fretboard, teaching him how to follow his own barre chords and explaining the bass-drum/note symbiosis. Bits and pieces of gear were crammed into the room week by week, threatening to crowd them all out by the end of May, but somehow they kept on rolling without a single argument or tantrum.

They were working in exactly the opposite way to Oasis: there was no established songwriter introducing structured material to be backed; all three were happy with more organic composition. To paraphrase Traffic, they were 'getting it together in the city', jamming and recording constantly, picking out the good lines and patterns at the end of the day, throwing them back into the melting pot the next. And this was how they liked it – their shared love of the Bunnymen and Joy Division, bands who loved the ensemble rather than one individual's vision, had taught them that these methods worked. The primitivism of Guigsy's bass in particular guaranteed a garage element to anything they did, however sophisticated Bonehead's chord progressions. Later, with the addition of a primal-force kind of drummer, 061 and its successors would benefit from having a rhythm section so rooted in crude power.

Guigs began to offer something else too, besides a pop-student's critical eye for what worked. He and Chris agreed to start collaborating on lyrics, which now took on a more rounded quality. The usual hassles associated with collaborative lyric-writing were absent – as best mates, with shared beliefs about Manchester, England and meaningful composition, they were perfectly suited for working together. And when Guigsy suggested that the name 061 was a tad too obvious and needed changing, Chris agreed without proprietal sulk. He had always believed that Guigs had good judgement, that his advice and encouragement would tend to be worth following. All three were quietly pleased with how they were progressing. They had proved to each other that there was something here worth working on. And if they needed any further encouragement to keep aiming for the stars from the gutter, they got it at the end of May – in the middle of the Mersey flats.

May 26, 1990: it's the eve of the Stone Roses' Spike Island concert and the lads are looking at the Bonemobile: 'Not very Madchester is it?' Tulsa Redneck chic, if there is such a thing, was hardly the ticket for Mancunium's epiphany. As in all things, follow the Roses – out came every can of paint available. Whatever the temptation to do a Revolver Records-style trash-job, they opted for a touch of Squirism; after a morning's solid artistry, the Bonemobile had been reborn as the Love Machine, a psychedelic tapestry. Burnage would be travelling to Widnes in style.

An advance guard of 30 went up that night, kipping in a farmer's field overnight. At 5 a.m., Chris, Bonehead and company set off, to be ready for the ultimate breakfast party in the Spike Island car park. Replace bacon with weed, tea with lager and eggs with Es and you get the idea. Music hacks from the *NME* and *Melody Maker* made a bee-line for the outrageous vehicle and its completely stoned campers, doing a picture-shoot of the Burnage boys for their Spike Island specials – little knowing that they had captured two members of the nineties' biggest band in their frame.

Guigs, Bonehead and Chris somehow managed to stick together all day, losing the rest in the delirium of the 30,000 crowd. They were obviously all off their faces but able to marvel at their inspirations on stage, doing everything they dreamed about. Somehow, they emerged at the front of the stage, where Bonehead's old mate Fonzo was going into one. The lads started shouting 'give us a gig' and, had they been given the slightest encouragement, would've mounted the podium and performed their four-song set. It was one of those occasions when, however stoned you are, the magic makes you feel empowered, capable of anything. They were all, to a man, buzzing off it for days to come.

It's become fashionable now to claim Spike Island wasn't much cop, at least when reviewed in the cold light of day. The organization was poor, the timing of the day's programme ill-conceived and some of the commercial activity too grasping. But the Burnage boys never wavered in their collective opinion that this was their greatest gig of all time. Knebworth, Earl's Court or Maine Road couldn't compare, for the Roses meant more at that moment than Oasis ever could. Those who've lived through both bands' careers will understand; those who haven't will have to take their word for it.

7

You've Got Everything Now

Spike Island acted upon the lads like a two-week
course of amphetamines, driving them to rehearse
harder, to write more, to tighten up, to get ambitious.
Farting around in someone's front room was now too
half-baked – they needed a proper gaff to really get
it together. But in Chris's and Bonehead's minds nig-
gled a tricky musical problem: Guigsy's bass-playing.
Comparing the head-swirling virtuosity of the Roses'
Mani to Guigsy's novice plodding-by-numbers was
instructive. At least Bonehead and Chris sounded like
the business. One afternoon, as Guigsy sweated over
a bass run which required some left-handed double-
digitation, Chris took the bass from him and rattled
the line off himself, almost without thinking. Bonehead broke into the ensuing pregnant pause with a
cheery grin: 'Perhaps Chris should switch to bass?'
Leaving Guigs on maracas, no doubt. Chris laughed
off the momentary embarrassment and handed back
the instrument to a relieved Guigsy. 'Nah, he'll get it

sorted – I'm staying singer.'

It had been another million-pound moment, for had Chris been hard-headed enough to take the logical step, Guigs would've disappeared from the Oasis story within days, leaving Chris to follow the inevitable path towards Oasis, stardom and riches. But Guigs was Chris's mate; he wasn't going to dump him now. Guigsy's natural intelligence and ruthless ambition would have made him a success in some other less exalted field. He could have become Oasis's Stu Sutcliffe, but Chris's generosity condemned himself to the eventual role of their Pete Best. Rock 'n' roll is no business for the nice guy.

They found their rehearsal room yards away. It would later be said that early Oasis were essentially a garage band, and it was literally the case: Chris Hutton's garage was where the Oasis sound really began to coalesce. It would be more than just a place to rehearse. By the time the Bonemobile had wheezed through its duties, dumping the garage's contents on the local tip before refilling with musical gear and creature comforts, the garage resembled a bijou club. No lad grows out of that 12-year-old compulsion to find a refuge free from women, parents and authority; any grown-up male club or society is surely nothing more than an extension of the kids' den, with booze, drugs and assorted adult pleasures replacing the penny chews, pop and underwear catalogues. The lads rifled through their houses and transplanted old carpets, tables and sofas, as well as robbed pub goodies such as pint-pots, ashtrays and barstools. (Nicking the latter unseen by landlord was a trick of Copperfield intricacy.) Within 48 hours, Club 061 was open for business.

The nightly routine was well-established for the group and their hangers-on. Last orders – leave pub – Club 061 – beer and weed frenzy – rehearse whilst still conscious. (And if you were going home to a shag afterwards, what more could any lad want from life?) Not only did the three boys feel more and more like a band, but they were now all good mates too, bonded together by chords, Boddies and shared spliffs.

Guiggsy gave them self-belief. He always knew he was going to be a success, at least monetarily. Every now and then, he'd gee the lads up, roaring them on with a shout of 'We're gonna be famous!' or 'This time in five years, we'll be millionaires, I'm tellin' ya.' If there was a Thatcherite tinge to his ambition, it was deliberate. Chris recalls walking down Market Street with him once, whereupon they were accosted by *Socialist Worker* sellers, mistaking the lads for fellow lefties. Guigs gave them a mouthful of splenetic right-wing invective, leading one SWP-er to ask 'Are you a Maggie boot-boy, then?' Guigs grinned and replied 'Yeah, what about it then?' He loved his Queen and country and always believed in looking after number one – a real eighties boy.

He even had that Tory weakness for big, hard leadership types. Chris remembers him being in thrall to local hardmen and boxers, attracted to dominance and power. As with many would-be self-made men in the eighties, he had no time for the English cult of carping at success. Victors were to be admired and learned from, not questioned. So even though he was a City fan, he spent as much time slavering over the Anfield Machine as venerating the Blues, telling any who'd listen to stop being bitter and appreciate the best instead. And Guigsy was always the king of footie bullshit, able to argue the toss about anything to do with the game – it was a natural extension of his gift for the blarney. In all these attitudes, you can see the drive that is necessary to get ahead in the music-biz – but also, in Chris's opinion, the hard-headed calculation that might allow him to abandon his friend for the greater glory of Guigs.

Bonehead was always the most popular in his crowd. To him, nothing should be taken too seriously; always stay game for a laugh and you'll be sorted. His insouciance, breezy optimism and general good humour were the perfect foil to Guigs' and Chris's occasional bouts of intensity and introspection. It made him a surprising success with the women too, as he garnered greater attention than either of his more hirsute colleagues by offering an irresistible combination of empathetic laughter and a nice bit of rough. (One hastens to add that he settled down once Kate arrived on the scene; in fact, by the time of their Manchester University gig in 1994, Guigs was telling Chris that the biggest draw for the groupies now was Noel.) He was always more of a rowdy beer-boy than a moody druggie, with a legendary ability to sleep anywhere, no matter how inappropriate the circumstances.

Yet his commitment to his music was never in doubt. He would always argue that rehearsals were unmissable, that devotion to the greater cause must be absolute. He would practise riffs and repeat for hours until his fingers were bleeding; you rarely saw him without some sort of rudimentary bandaging on his hands. And if he slipped below his standards, cheeky charm would see him through. On the night of Bryan Robson's testimonial, Chris still turned up for rehearsals, knowing how tough Bonehead was on commitment. But Bone never showed. Next day, he swanned in to explain that he'd not only been to the game, but that his mate had caught Robbo's boots when they were flung into the crowd. As Chris, loyal Red, gaped open-mouthed in jealousy and annoyance, Bonehead grinned sheepishly and shrugged. Chris just shook his head and laughed – what could you do? That was Bonehead for you. All in all, the chemistry between the three seemed to Chris to be spot on. Indeed, he can't remember the trio ever getting into one serious argument during their entire time together.

All they needed now was a new name, ready for the first low-key gig Chris had arranged at Withington's Bridge club. As they talked one night, lounging about amidst a sea of bottles and cans with the garage door open, it began to rain. 'What about "The Rain"?' remarked Chris. 'Yeah, what about it?' answered Bonehead as the drizzle turned to pelting sheets.

'No, I mean "The Rain",' persisted Chris. The three looked at each other, murmured the name and agreed in an instant. For a band which sought to represent the Mancunian experience, and whose sound owed much to the city's doomy rock tradition of wet greatcoats and cold riffs, it was deemed perfect. In good Manc style, it both took the piss out of, and yet celebrated, the city's image simultaneously.

Hewitt, like others, didn't research any of this properly and declared that the group were simply called 'Rain'. He somehow came up with the notion that the lads had named the group after the Lennon song which backed *Paperback Writer*. Perhaps this was part of the Beatles bullshit fed to him by Oasis members, all of whom now seek to build up the Fab Four's role in their lives. Actually, the Beatles meant almost nothing to the Rain: too pop, too Scouse, too old. Guigsy, according to Hewitt, discovered the Beatles via his mother's repetitive spinning of the *Love Songs* compilation, but Chris never heard Guigs mention the Beatles once in all the time he knew him. Bonehead never seemed to have any retro influences, bar those picked up second-hand from his brother, and in any event preferred working methods more like the Stones' than the Beatles'. Chris simply didn't own any Beatles records at all; his heroes were all his near-contemporaries. Noel too, as his brother Paul inadvertently confirms when listing his siblings's tastes in *Brothers*, never appeared to talk about the Beatles and certainly never obsessed over them as a teenager in the way that he did over, say, Easterhouse or the Smiths.

In fact, it is an absolute mystery as to how the Beatles came to take such a hold over the Gallaghers and Oasis. Mancunian pop and rock has largely been untouched by direct Beatlepower, which has tended to affect Liverpool, Birmingham and London much more notably. Since the Hollies, only 10cc and the Buzzcocks have shown any real sign of Beatlism in either their working methods or output. Even the Roses, whose pop sensibilities were greater than any modern Manchester band before Oasis, were remarkably free of Merseybeat quirks once they'd hit their mark. Slack writers who talked of Beatle influences on the Roses album should have said sixties influences: you can hear the Byrds, Simon and Garfunkel, the Doors, Love and even Manfred Mann, but not the Beatles to any proper degree.

As late as 89/90, when Noel was about to disappear from Burnage on Inspirals duty, none of his contemporaries could see any sort of Lennonism in him. At The Packhorse, Noel would put the Who or the Roses on the jukebox, but never the Beatles. Chris remembers that the early Noel songs he heard on that demo tape bore not a trace of Lennon/McCartney influence. If we take on trust Hewitt's assertion that Noel turned Guigsy onto late Beatles stuff like 'I am the Walrus', then we have to deduce that such influences emerged fairly late in the day, for both of them; indeed, Guigsy never spent any time at all with Noel until after he took over Oasis. The suspicion remains that the

Beatles became a useful template for Noel and the rest, rather than being a pre-existing life-shaping force.

Because Beatles songs and methods were a largely untapped source in late eighties/early nineties Manchester, they offered Noel a source of mock-originality: aping the Beatles, and presumably discovering that he could write Beatlesque songs, did at least mark out Noel and his band as being different from their contemporary rivals. When everyone else in Manchester – including the pre-Noel Rain – sounded like the Roses, Mondays or some baggy combination, Oasis's hardening of the La's/Beatles sound drew deserved attention. The public's desire for the return of 'The Song', which a smart operator like Noel couldn't fail to have spotted, chimed in perfectly with his Masterplan, as did Manchester's proud provincial desire for a Roses replacement. By the time Blur and Suede had opened up the British market for the post-Nirvana guitar-pop renaissance, Oasis would be ready to step in for the absent Roses.

Whatever desires the Rain possessed didn't impress their neighbour much. A few weeks of clattering cacophony from the garage soon had him on the blower to the local bill, after his attempt at personal intervention had faltered upon the sight of ten tanked-up, piss-taking lads greeting him at the garage door. Labouring under police instructions to halve the volume or be nicked, the Rain's residence at Club 061 would surely have to be terminated. Bonehead came to the rescue: his big-shot brother Martin was going to

L.A. to build some mixing desks. They could rehearse full blast at his place, right up until the date of their gig which, by sweet coincidence, would be the night Martin returned. The Rain would be ready to debut after all.

The gig posters said 'Special Guests 061' – they hadn't managed to tell Tony French about the name change quickly enough. Still, he'd done a good job on them and was happy to get involved in any design work the band would need. At the height of the Manchester T-shirt phenomenon, they'd need someone with a good eye and flair if they were to spread the word about the band and make a few non-declared quid on the side. Every would-be popster in town knew the line about the Inspirals: that they supposedly made more money from Moo! T-shirts than they did from records.

Chris had chosen the night carefully: his missus and sisters were having their birthday party at the club, so the place would be crawling with friends and well-wishers. When you're taking your first nervous steps, you don't want the extra hassle of dodging flying beer bottles. And nervous they were, too: Guigs and Bonehead turned 'arsebackers', too shy and unsure to face the crowd full-on. Bonehead, although he'd gigged before, hadn't been out in public with a band for a couple of years. It was almost touching to see such a veteran get the butterflies as much as the novice Guigsy. It fell to Chris, as singer, to front it out. And despite the dodgy sound, he performed for the best part of 30 minutes as his band-mates cowered in the shadows, hammering out three lengthy Joy Division-style songs.

For Chris, *performing* meant more than just singing – he had no time for the static arrogance later employed by his successor. 'Frontman' meant a requirement to move, exhort, enthuse and express. Months of practice on pub tables and in the garage came good. 'He's off 'is 'ead' was the common verdict of the crowd – and they were loving it. For a first performance, the reception was excellent, and Chris came off stage knowing that he could do this lark. He could be a singer; he could be a contender.

But in the meantime, a human drummer wouldn't go amiss. You don't play Spike Island with an Echo behind you. A relieved post-gig Guigsy, who'd managed to get through without making any major blunders, was fired-up now: 'Let's get Tony Mac in, let's go for it.' Chris knew Tony McCarroll from way back – a 'plastic Paddy' some said, but a good bloke and a regular down on the footie fields most weekends. Someone said he was around the area, working on the roads as a navvy. As soon as they could get hold of Tony, they'd pitch the job to him. The rhythm section that would conquer the continent would then be complete.

The lads were buzzing now, rushing ahead of themselves, wanting the world yesterday. The Milestone, their second home, had offered a gig for July 11: rather than wait for Tony Mac, they decided to go ahead and play it. Not only that – they resolved to play one of the big cards up their sleeves. Burnage's most famous resident lived just around the corner from Chris and was a hero to all three lads: Andy Rourke, the Smiths' bassist. They'd seen him down the Milestone with his missus a couple of times, so why not invite him to the gig, have a drink and see if he could help them get ahead? A couple of years later, Johnny Marr would perform a similar service for Noel's Oasis, an event sometimes written up as a liaison which would've been beyond the reach of 'no-hopers' like the Rain. Nowadays, no one in the Oasis entourage wants to admit that Chris Hutton could have secured similar patronage and Rourke's involvement in the Oasis story has been strangely ignored. As we shall see, that is enormously misleading: without the Rourke link-up, the Rain might never have progressed to the stage where they became Oasis.

All three agreed that approaching Andy would be a top move. But as the Bonemobile chugged down the road towards his house, no one wanted to make the actual contact. To a man, they were shitting it. After all, this wasn't just some industry head or media hack but a real live Smith. Co-creator of the records they'd all venerated for years. Stage performer whom they'd all worshipped in the flesh at so many a gig. All right, so he wasn't Morrissey, but he was the biggest name by far any of them had ever had the chance to meet. 'You knock on.' 'Fuck off, you do it, you're the oldest.' 'Look, this group was your idea, you do it.' 'No way, he's the fuckin' bass player, he can go.' (And so on for ten minutes.) Eventually, Chris went, the lone frontman amidst arsebackers. Doorbell rings, palms sweating. A Smith, in the flesh, answers. Chris is speechless for about three seconds. Gold discs glint on the hallway walls. The spikey hair's changed but it's him, the one who's looked out at him from the gatefold of his well-worn *Hatful of Hollow* all these years. Chris manages to blurt out: 'Erm-hello-my-band's-playing-at-the-Milestone-can-you-come-and-see-what-you-think-erm-please-erm-thanks.'

Chris had almost begun to turn away, fully expecting the 'Sorry, I'm too busy' line. Instead, Andy grinned, said 'Sure, see you there' and asked for the date. The lads took the rest of the day off, for general buzzing and back-slapping.

When Chris and the lads walked into the Milestone on the night of the 11th, they knew they were on their way. The place was absolutely heaving, crammed wall-to-wall with Madchester kids who were even standing on the bar and in the fireplace. They had always wanted to be a local band built on local support – now here it was for the taking. Today Burnage, tomorrow Manchester, next day Britain . . . it's always been the ideologically sound way. As Noel later remarked, we all seek to be a band that comes from 'the street', not from an imposed concept. The reader can judge whether Oasis merit that description as much as the Rain.

One of the lads they knew in the audience had a camera, recording the whole event for posterity, though clearly not expecting part of a world-beating band of the future to be captured on film. Even better: both Andy Rourke and Tony McCarroll were in. Chris gripped Tony before they went on: 'Do you wanna be in with us?' Tony, knowing that as a scarce resource he had the whip-hand, held back for the moment, saying he'd see what they were like during the gig before deciding. The band would be auditioning for the drummer! Whoever complains about the way drummers are supposedly denigrated in the music-biz (e.g. 'What do you call a non-musician on a tour-bus? The drummer') has forgotten how the balance of power lies at the grassroots . . .

Suitably inspired by their situation, the boys went for it big-style. Arsebacking, for one, was history. Chris was especially manic, responding to the crowd's raucous hollering like a time-served trouper, going with the flow of the soaring atmosphere. The consensus afterwards was that it had been 'a wild one', capped by a thorough trashing of the clichéd 'Wild Thing'. Chris hadn't wanted to do it, but he was outvoted: 'Always do a cover when you're new,' advised Guigsy, ever the pragmatist. 'All right,' concurred Chris, 'but only if I can turn it into a weed song.' Guigsy enthused over the idea, egging him on as Chris injected over-the-top drugged-out lyrics to the verses of the old warhorse. The crowd, half of whom were semi-stoned, loved it. Andy Rourke came over at the end to say it had been 'funny as fuck' and stayed to join in the drinks session.

Later Chris would review the video and cringe at his performance, 'swinging the mike and Brown-ing about like a monkey on acid' as he puts it, but his antics seemed to have done the business with the punters. Besides, when he felt like 'going into one', nothing could stop him anyway; it wasn't calculated but natural. Losing yourself in the music, as Ian Curtis's example had taught him, was never anything to apologize for, no matter how much of a dick you look on the video. Go check Curtis doing 'Transmission' on *The Old Grey Whistle Test* for illustration.

They'd certainly passed Tony Mac's audition, anyway: the drummer hared over to their table to pledge himself to the group and was down at their garage with his bongos within hours. 'I'll be round with the kit on Saturday,' said Tony as he departed – three lads messing about with guitars had now, at last, become a band. They'd tackle the problem of where the fuck to put his drums ('On the roof?') when they'd sobered up.

Another lucky break: a couple of mates were in a band called Reluctance, looking for someone to share rehearsal room costs. Chris jumped in quick, and by the weekend the Rain, complete with drummer and full kit, were happily ensconced in Stockport's Green Rooms Studios. The lads played through their five completed original songs without Tony, allowing him to listen and work out the patterns and movement. After a couple of hours, they could all play through as an ensemble and the three founders realized what they'd been missing. For a while in the eighties, the technocrats lectured us that the drummer was dead, inevitably to be replaced by the machine. Hearing Tony bring their songs to life, adding new dimensions and rhythmic

ideas throughout, took them all to a new high. To give
the nineties' Dad-rockers credit, they've exposed the
stupidity of those tech-head arguments in many areas,
but none more so than on the question of percussion.
You simply cannot beat or replace the real thing. And
Tony, a true tub-thumper of primal energetic force, was
the real thing. Nobody ever claimed he was a technician
of Steve White class, but the character assassination he
has undergone since leaving Oasis is a disgrace. He was
exactly the right kind of drummer for both the Rain
and early Oasis – and, given their continued rhythmic
simplicity, for later Oasis too.

For the first time, the members of the Rain felt they
had original material to believe in; all three contributors to the writing found new confidence in their own
abilities. The trickle of songs would turn into a flood –
copyright McGuigan-Hutton-Arthurs.

8

Strangeways Here We Come

The song 'Rooftop Rave', about the Strangeways Prison
riot and siege, was a good example of the Rain's
determination to reflect the life and concerns of their
own city, and to make it clear on which side of
Thatcherite Britain's social battle-lines they stood.
That April explosion inside Manchester's notorious
Victorian jail dominated the national media for 25 days,
yet the coverage was such that an outsider would not
have comprehended the impact it made, particularly
upon the city's working classes. This was an issue,
more than the clichéd North/South or have/have-not
divides, which determined whether you were 'one of
us' or part of 'the enemy within', to adopt Thatcherite
terminology. It cut across standard political allegiances,
becoming that terribly old-fashioned phenomenon: an
issue of class. Guigsy, and to a lesser extent Bonehead,
would normally take a Toryish view of politics, Guigsy
especially being a fervent admirer of Mrs T. Yet the

riot united the band, dissolving their differing party-
political beliefs; their sympathies were entirely with
the prisoners.

Not so Middle England, the Establishment, the women
who read the *Daily Mail*, the *Sun*'s editorial team . . . all
quivered with horror and outrage as events unfolded.
This was their nightmare: the underclass acting in
solidarity, defying the power of the state, refusing
to suffer in silence. Those who railed most against
the prisoners had no understanding of penal policy
or the conditions inside the crumbling system. Most
apparently couldn't care either; wasn't this what the
Home Office collected part of their taxes for, to shut
these people away and keep them controlled, so that
'decent folk' would never have to think about such
sordidness?

From a Mancunian, working-class point of view,
that April had a very different perspective. In that
urban community, it is now much easier to find
someone who has either been in the nick, been in
danger of it, or been close to someone who's been
inside, than it is to find someone who is completely
'untainted' by prison. The *Daily Mail* reader may not
care that eighteen-year-olds hang themselves in prison
every week, or that innocent men may serve a year on
remand, or that assaults by staff on prisoners generally
go unpunished – but for some, that might be their son
or husband in there, whether actually or potentially.
As soon as Strangeways went off, thousands of local
people immediately connected to it emotionally and

intellectually. The boys in the Rain were just four of them.

Understandably, there was also the visceral excitement of such an enormous news event kicking off within sight of the city centre, and of the vibrancy of the roof-top protests themselves. As the Rain's gleeful refrain ran: 'See Paul Taylor on the roof / Playing a tune on his guitar / What about the rest of the boys? / They're havin' a rave on the roof!' The visual impact alone was extraordinary. For a month, you could take an hour off shopping, walk the five minutes up to Strangeways, and if lucky catch the matinée performance of slate-chucking, water-cannon and defiant ghetto-blasted obscenities. To be flippant, it was the best show in town.

There was a certain pride too in the rash of riots that broke out across the nation that month, all inspired by the bravery and solidarity on show at Strangeways. Just as we had with Madchester, we were leading the rest of the nation towards progress. For Strangeways undoubtedly kicked the Home Office and Prison Service out of its revolting complacency and reversed a savage drift towards penal Dickensianism. For years afterwards, 'Avoiding another Strangeways' was a mantra to be heard whenever prison policy was discussed within the Establishment. A prison riot, like a street riot, reminds authority of its limits. They are almost always wholly beneficial events, except for the poor sods who get scapegoated. They teach warders not to behave like bootboys, home secretaries to stop posturing as hardmen to the media and the Home Office to remember they're dealing with humans, not animals. When the final five came down on the cherrypicker on 25 April, they knew they faced retribution, severe punishment and probably a whitewashed inquiry: indeed, they got all three. Whether viewed as heroes or anti-heroes, they had at least made a point that would never be forgotten by any who lived in Manchester at the time, nor by the authorities whose noses they had so spectacularly bloodied. The bleating of the prison officers who served there should be ignored. The nick was without doubt one of the worst three of its type in Britain, a status owed as much to some of its staff, who'd made Strangeways an infamous 'screw's nick', as to any higher administrative deficiencies. A brief reminder of what this HMP allowed, courtesy of Eric Allison's *Strangeways 1990*: 'To go down to the block ... to see men beaten black and blue, men cowering naked in a corner of a strip cell, men in obscene body-belts, lying stinking in their own urine and excreta ... D1 was a huge festering sore, a prison within a prison, where men could be viciously abused and the perpetrators be confident their crimes would never come to light.'

The Woolf Inquiry report was an anaemic joke, of course, as the inquiry saw fit not to hear from the prisoners or allow them to be represented properly; its conclusion should have been that not only did

Strangeways deserve to burn but the 'vandals' should have been congratulated for bringing the scandal to the nation's attention. And the Rain, in tribute, played 'Rooftop Rave' at every gig; it was perhaps their most memorable and popular song.

9

The Death of a
Disco Dancer

Madchester by Stefan Pierlejewski

As the speakers squeezed the air around us, the crowd erupted. The metallic clangs and bleeps echoed around our heads and, all at once, we were rocking and jumping in unison to the sound of A Guy Called Gerald. It was the Haçienda's final 'Hot' night and the place was rammed. There was an electricity in the air that summed up what exactly had been growing for the last couple of years. Warehouse parties, house parties, parties in fields — in fact any plot of land or building we could get our sweaty hands on where the cost was low, the drinks were soft and the dress code was non-existent.

There had been a rapid climb in numbers of partygoers since the scene started to blossom towards the end of '86. Detroit and Chicago house music had been steadily infiltrating Britain for a number of years, even to the point of charting

(Darryl Pandy's classic 'Love Can't Turn Around' for example). It had emerged from the dying embers of the Disco scene and been given new life by technological advances.

Programmable drum machines and cheap synths had taken hold and brought with them a breath of fresh air for the wealth of financially challenged talent, who had been waiting patiently in the wings for their 15 minutes of fame. Already something weird was happening. A genetic mutation had occurred in the laboratory that was 'house'. The bastard son of Disco outstretched its hand to the chemical cupboard, and swallowed hard. The sound of Acid House was born ... and it was heading straight for Manchester.

LSD was back in a big way. Not since the sixties had production been so big or in such demand. Exploration in club surrealism was the order of the day, and who was I to argue? There was a tight synergy between electronic sound and acid, and more and more people seemed to be catching on. There was this strange hybrid of sound that had more to do with rhythm and frequency than it did music. It required abusing old equipment in strange ways to create new techniques. Repetition was used to create a trance-like, hypnotic state, bending and twisting the frequencies so they formed new timbres, new shapes and, most important, new journeys.

To anyone but the chemically induced, this seemed a mindless, irritating waste of vinyl, but to those in the know it was science, art even. We had discovered something totally new. There were no guitars, no singers, no band and no hero worship. The music was anonymous yet enthralling and our parents fucking hated it!

There was a problem though: it was all so new that there wasn't much of it about. There were a limited number of clubs in Manchester geared up to the quality of sound and lighting that Acid House consumption required. There was more fun to be had in people's front rooms and cellars than any glitzy club. We needed more space, better sound, superior lighting, well ... just more.

Then the news came.

Before we knew what was happening there were six of us crammed into a small car tearing down the M1 with just a blotter of acid, 60 quid and a giant adrenaline rush between us. We had heard about a large Acid House party, down south, with a 50-kilowatt sound-system and we were virtually pissing ourselves at the prospect. This is what we had been waiting for the last six months. It was going to be like Ken Kesey's Acid Test but timewarped 20 years into the future; and we could hardly sit still long enough to drive.

We arrived at eleven o'clock at night, to a huge queue of cars, followed by a gateway. Our excitement got the better of us and we decided to just ditch the car and head up the track to see what awaited us for the night. Nothing, and I really mean nothing, prepared us for the absolute joy of what we saw. An airplane hangar! ... We were totally speechless for abut 30 seconds and then tentatively approached this massive, writhing throng. There were literally thousands of people there, all totally tripped out of their brains. One bog-eyed goon politely asked us for what suddenly seemed a very meagre ten-pound entrance fee and we were in.

The sound was unbelievable. Towering above us at the end of the hangar were two black skyscrapers of sound.

Between them, beaming precise geometric patterns through the crowd, was the biggest and most colourful laser we had ever seen. We took one look at each other and fell about in heaps of laughter at our incredible fortune. I should perhaps mention at this point that the rather large blotter of acid we had previously divided had just started to kick in ... big style.

Needless to say the rest of the night was a euphoric and twisted blur. Our minds and bodies were entirely taken over for eight hours and every minute of it was total pleasure. There was a safety to be gained amongst the writhing mass of fellow trippers. Everyone jacked and spasmed amongst each other, part unaware, part hyper-aware of their fellow beings. Most were too lost within themselves and their trip to notice anything at all. Words fail really, so ...

Gradually, as the light invaded our colourful darkness, we sloped off, one by one, to await our fate back in the outside world. Only the walking wounded and the criminally insane remained, shuffling and dragging their feet, jaws slack and eyes rolling. It was all too reminiscent of a scene from *One Flew Over The Cuckoo's Nest* for my liking. The daylight has a habit of cruelly unveiling reality.

The journey back to Manchester was a long one. Half-crippled by eight hours' dancing and one almighty acid come-down, we re-lived the night's events with some sense of folklore. Even in our state of collective wreckage we were already hungry for more.

We were still bemoaning the lack of activity in Manchester as we gathered at our local later on that day. Still enthused by the previous night's activity, we tried to imagine a solution to the problem of our fixation. How long would we have to wait before we could satisfy our psychedelic hunger for more?

'I take it you guys haven't heard about Blackburn then?' said a rather dodgy dealer-type as he leaned over our table.

Blackburn? What the fuck did that backwater have to do with anything? Is this guy taking the piss?

'Sorry mate, what was that?' I paraphrased my thoughts, rather sensibly considering his size.

'I said, I take it you haven't heard about the parties they've been putting on in Blackburn. Huge fuckers, in warehouses like?' he repeated.

We all looked gormlessly at each other, half-disbelieving, half-excited. He proceeded to tell us all about these parties, what went on, who was running them and most importantly where the next one was likely to be. They sounded amazing, just what we had been hoping for. Two whole weeks: how the hell were we going to wait that long? This was worse than waiting for Christmas when you're a kid.

The days soon passed and before we knew it Saturday was upon us again. Eager for an enhanced good time, the daytime was taken up with trying to score some goodies for the weekend (this was to become standard practice for thousands) and frantically telephoning a number on a flyer we had been given in order to get directions. The evening came and we were once again shooting up the motorway, adrenaline buzzing. One strange thing that did occur to us was that there was a rather large amount of car activity heading in the same general direction. I was too busy skinning-up to notice that the occupants of these vessels all looked remarkably like Manchester scallies, as excited as we were.

We got to the M6 turn-off for Blackburn and at the round-about, converging from every direction imaginable, were cars! Hundreds, maybe thousands of cars, all containing partygoers! I had never seen anything like it in my life. All the way up the hill, as far as the eye could see, into Blackburn, cars totally blocked the road, bumper to bumper. In every single car were crammed party people. Our brains raced to try and add up roughly how many people this would amount to at the party, but after several minutes we decided we were far too stoned to see, let alone count, and promptly gave up.

Where did all these people come from? How did they all get to hear about this? Was there a secret network that we knew nothing about? Why was the moon so big? Why were my hands growing lizard scales?

'What the fuck is going on?' I shouted.

Sniggers followed.

'What the fuck is going on?' I repeated, turning to the driver, who now had an overblown balloon for a head. I realized that I wasn't going to get any sense out of a man without a mouth, and so as our car was at a standstill, I thought I would go and ask the people in the car in front of us.

'Excuse me,' I said, tapping on their car window, 'Why are my hands growing lizard scales?'

A very angry wolfman hurriedly wound down the window, hairy nostrils flaring wildly, and started mouthing words in no apparent order. All I could notice was that his tongue kept flapping and falling out from his mouth.

I hurried back to the car as fast as my legs would carry

me, making sure that I locked the door and all the others in the car behind me.

'Acid coming on yet?' someone asked.

Of course! I suddenly felt extremely relieved, not to mention slightly embarrassed. Acid has this way of creeping up on you, to the point sometimes that you can forget that you've taken any at all.

'Thank God for that,' I said. 'I thought I was going mad for a minute.'

'Perhaps you are ...' someone helpfully reassured.

Safe in the knowledge that I wasn't going to end up in the asylum I buckled up and waited for the traffic jam to subside. It took hours. We managed to trawl every nook and cranny of the streets to Blackburn until we reached a warehouse in the middle of an industrial estate. There were hundreds of people queuing outside a small door. From the outside we could hear the throbbing bass. It took perhaps another 20 minutes to get through the queue and then we had joined the 5,000. It was like a breath of fresh air, from life on the outside. Getting involved in a party is a bit like going on holiday for two weeks. You finally get home, exhausted from your journey, but totally refreshed from the overall trip. We had just arrived at our holiday destination and we were going to make the most of every minute of it.

The crowd and the music were pulsing but strangely, unlike the party down south, everyone was smiling, grinning like the cat that had found the cream. There was something about this that gave the party a boost. It was infectious. Soon enough we were dancing about, smiling while we absorbed the artificial sunshine that the lighting provided. For once we did not feel isolated from the rest of the people at the party. Strangers approached offering water, chewing gum and oddly, conversation. Frustratingly in my acid haze, I could barely communicate with any of them, bar the odd grunt and rubbery smile. However, this didn't seem to matter. Nobody seemed to disapprove of my temporary mental and social incapacity, they just shook my hand furiously and said things like 'Have a good one, mate.'

So the 'Second Summer of Love' began. It was June 1988 and the Blackburn party scene took over the North. For us and thousands of others, jaunts up to Blackburn became a thing of regularity. Every weekend, somewhere in Blackburn, there was a party to go to. Sometimes it would be after club hours but mostly it was the place to be. No one thought twice about the endless traffic queues and dodges with the police, it became part and parcel of the experience. It was a cat-and-mouse game with the authorities ... and the ravers were winning.

By this time Manchester was blossoming. Clubs, bars and shops were changing to accommodate this new breed that required a lifestyle and fashion of its own. Record shops began appearing, taking advantage of the new clientele and providing an extremely valuable service for the hungry new breed of DJs (of which there were a rapidly growing number).

Perhaps the most famous and long-lasting of these was Eastern Bloc records, which occupied a small, lower corner of a soon-to-be-notorious place called Affleck's Palace. Eastern Bloc was owned by part of a then small, underground Manchester dance group who used it to finance their studio time. The band were called 808 State. This turned out to be a very shrewd move on their part. The shop began to do so well that they helped finance other Manchester bands like A Guy Called Gerald and the Inspiral Carpets as well as gaining a massive reputation for themselves the world over.

The Haçienda, the club owned by New Order, was also gaining a large reputation. They regularly put on excellent nights of dance music, increasing as the dance scene grew, often marking changes in the scene with the closure of a successful night, never afraid to move on, with a new improved night of a different name and style appearing. Another night for those in the know was Konspiracy. This perhaps had its finger closest to the pulse of the Acid House movement. (Many an old Manc raver will often look back on these nights with watery eyes and great affection if prompted.) Soon the only night in Manchester unavailable for partying was Tuesday. But this was occupied by Manchester's finest and funniest underground radio programme, the 808 State show on the pirate Sunset Radio. It was a chance for the dance posse to keep up to date with what was going on and what was going to be on, in and around the area. It was also a chance to boost the ever-needed tape collection, with recordings of some of the finest white labels and hard-to-get imports.

There was once again a buzz about the city and not all of it to do with dance music. There were a few bands around that had taken what inspiration they needed from the dance culture and fused it with their own brand of guitar-driven songs, and people were starting to take serious note, especially the journalists. The two most talked-about bands (in case you have been living in a timewarp) were the Stone Roses and the Happy Mondays. Members of both bands were regularly seen at various nights at the Haçienda and occasionally at free parties (usually in the kind of state that you'd expect). Gone was the sombreness of the Smiths and out came something with more of a groove. There came a time when even clubbers would go and see their gigs and buy the records.

The Mondays were perhaps the most respected by ravers because of their uncannily similar attitude and general downright funk, but both bands gave Manchester its edge, its world notoriety and sadly, its new title ... MADchester.

Meanwhile back in the bizarre outer limits of Acid House things were changing. As the Haçienda's fantastic final Hot night drew to a close, the pied piper began to get more driving, emotional and downright sexy. Little did we know that we were about to find out why.

The bass was shaking and the crowd were going mental. There was something new in town and I was excitedly holding it in the palm of my sweaty hand. I took one last look at it before I flung my head back and swallowed. I shuffled around nervously, not quite knowing what to expect, and waited for it to kick in. My friends were in a similar predicament. It was the weekend that we hadn't been able to score our usual blotter of acid and, in the hope of finding some later, had gone on to Blackburn anyway. Despite using all the contacts at the party we could and whispering requests to every dodgy-looking reveller there was, we still came up with nothing.

'Only Es,' kept coming the reply. Since I didn't know what the hell they were talking about and not wanting to appear stupid, I declined and returned to my friends. 'What the fuck are Es? Anyone know?' Everyone looked blankly back at me. After five more minutes of sobriety the collective decision was to go and buy one anyway and inspect it. Several minutes later the elected purchaser came scurrying back with nothing.

'Twelve fucking quid man!' he said, as if he had just been asked if he required an enema. We were used to the cost of acid, which was only ever five pounds at the most and that was usually between two. Desperate times called for desperate measures, so we dug deep into our pockets and looking at the results decided to split two Es between four of us and just hope for the best. The best was exactly what we got.

Shulgin's 'baby acid' was better known as Ecstasy. It was to become the staple weekend diet of milions over the next eight years. If it had not appeared I doubt dance music would have been the formidable force that it is today. Like it or not, music and drugs have gone hand in hand for decades and the recent discovery of Ecstasy was no exception. It changed everybody's attitude. Seemingly overnight Manchester changed for the better (at least in the short term). Ecstasy has amazing properties. First, it causes an empathy with your surrounding fellow beings, which often turns to feelings of intense love. Second, it makes you want to dance your tits off.

As I plopped into the E bubble the phenomenal power of the bass caught me and I was powerless to resist. What felt like marshmallows instead of feet began to bounce and I felt lighter and more locked into the groove than I had ever done before. My whole body felt every beat in the music and by the looks of everyone else, my other three reprobate partners included, they all felt the same. There were grins from ear to ear littering the dancefloor. Wild happiness replaced, even replicated, the hallucinations. For the first time I understood the friendliness that we had previously encountered. The colours and the sound had an apparent purity that I had not experienced before and there were none of the distracting visuals or possible 'bad trips' previously associated with LSD. Every part of my being just felt so damned good.

Ecstasy was the final piece of the jigsaw in the puzzle that was Madchester.

During 1989 and 1990 Manchester's popularity rocketed. It was virtually all the press was writing about. Manchester had all the top bands: Stone Roses, Happy Mondays, New Order, 808 State, Inspiral Carpets and N-Joi. The Haçienda and Eastern Bloc had reached near legendary status and people were flocking to Manchester as if the Holy Grail were here. Even Manchester University was receiving thousands more student applications than it had ever had before as potential students rushed to become part of the thriving scene. Everyone in Manchester seemed to become a caricature: baggy trousers, trainers, fishing hats and a severe accent. 'Nice one' annoyingly became Manchester's most used phrase. Anyone who lived in Manchester suddenly became Mancunian whether they were from Devon or Glasgow and nearly everyone shopped at Afflecks Arcade.

A now well-known DJ called Sasha became king of the hill as he wowed herds of revellers on a regular basis. The parties in Blackburn continued to thrive except attendance was becoming ridiculous. This did nothing to help the problems with the police or the tabloid press. It became harder and harder to simply tap into lampposts for the power supply or break into disused warehouses for the party. However, organizers and partygoers always seemed to be one step ahead. It felt for a while in Manchester like nothing could stop us. Sadly this was not to last forever.

On April 27, 1990 a bill to make warehouse parties illegal was passed. It gave the police new powers of arrest and was the first nail in the coffin for the Manchester party scene. The second followed only a month later in May, when the police tried to revoke the Haçienda's licence in order to shut it down. They were all too well aware of the scale of the club's drug consumption and, following an earlier 'E fatality' in July 1989, had finally decided to do something about it. The Haçienda narrowly managed to survive this on the promise of good behaviour. However, the attraction of the club's popularity had brought in the Manchester gangs, which created enough problems of its own. The Haçienda finally closed of its own accord in January 1991, a few days after the New Year celebrations, following gang threats and in particular the threatening of a bouncer with a loaded firearm. Things were not looking good.

It seemed like Madchester was finally being consigned to the asylum. The press had begun its backlash. The Roses had disappeared into oblivion, following their 'Fools Gold' success and label difficulties, and Shaun Ryder, the Mondays' frontman, was rumoured to have entered rehab. In May 1991 the Haçienda reopened but the pride was short-lived when, after only a few weeks, six bouncers were reportedly attacked with a machete.

Madchester had become better known as Gunchester and the crown was seemingly passed onto the next set of deserving mortals. There were constant arrests back in the party world of both organizers and dealers as police struggled to enforce their authority. It became utterly impossible to freely put on or enjoy a party that was not a fully licensed event; and the authorities were doing their damnedest to make sure those licences were not given out. Partygoers began to get bored with the sheer difficulty of trying to have a good time and eventually went to seek entertainment elsewhere.

House was croaking. But for a while, just for a while, we had been kings of the wildest frontier. For now though the party was well and truly over ... at least till the next time.

10

These Things Take Time

With Tony Mac in the bag, the Rain felt confident enough in their future to undergo the rite of passage every modern Manc band has known: the trip to Johnny Roadhouse. Oxford Road's legendary music shop has only one challenger in town – A1 music at the good end of Oxford Road – but Johnny's was always the place to go for your first kitting-out, due to the vast amount of decent second-hand gear on offer. Every Manc rock legend has trod its dusty floorboards and sifted through the piles of guitars and recording gizmos, searching for that enduring bargain which might just take you all the way to *Top of the Pops*. Guigs symbolically sealed his position in the band for good as he bought his first bass; Chris splashed out on a top-notch mike and stand; and Bonehead finally replaced his battered leads and connections. Most importantly, he snaffled himself a robust distortion unit – one flick of the switch, and he had instant guitar roar. Listening to their old demos, you can hear the change from that date: suddenly, with the drums and bass locked together in neo-punk tandem and Bone's guitar crashing brutally around the mix, the Rain and early Oasis were synonymous in sound, if not in song.

As the boys buzzed like kids who'd cleaned out a Mr Whippy's, Chris pulled out another joker from the pack: 'Remember Rosy, the DJ at Times Square? He reckons we're top – says we can gig there when we're ready.' Rosy was a mate of Chris's missus, the Times Square an excellent Didsbury venue. Respect was due to Chris, then – and Guigsy immediately responded with his own little coup.

Next day, as Chris enjoyed his Sunday lie-in, Guigs phoned: 'Chris, I'm at the Raffles Hotel on Anson Road.' 'What the fuck are you doing there on a Sunday morning?' Chris demanded blearily. 'Erm, I've copped off with the hotel manageress,' replied Guigs, trying not to sound too pleased with himself. Guigs hadn't exactly got a Liam-like reputation for pulling power. 'Anyway, I told her about the band and she said we can rehearse in the cellars in the sister hotel next door.' 'How much?' asked Chris. 'Nish,' grinned Guigs, 'we can stay there as long as we like for nish.' And verily Chris gave thanks: 'So there is a God, after all.'

They couldn't get down there fast enough next day. Just as Guigsy promised, the girl was sorted; Chris winked his congratulations to his mate. As for the cellars, they were more than they'd ever expected. Vast, good acoustics, and the boys would have their own keys to come and go as they pleased. Any time they fancied sinking a few jars, they simply had to nip upstairs to the patrons' bar, which they spent the rest of the day sampling in celebratory style. They'd have six weeks to get into shape for their first, all-band gig on September 5.

Tony French designed and produced a limited edition of 100 the Rain T-shirts, to be carefully spread about the area before the gig; enough to be noticed, not enough to be too available. They sold out in ten days and simply featured the legend 'Listen To The Rain'. (The T-shirts now sell in Japan for up to £200 a throw.) Purposefully, they kept publicity low-key, just enough of a murmur to ensure that their Milestone regulars and those in-the-know in Didsbury would turn up on the night. Whatever their level of self-confidence, they all appreciated that they couldn't oversell what would be their first real gig as a band.

Their own songs were panning out surprisingly well, benefiting from the fact that they'd been constructed co-operatively rather than imposed. Bonehead, as ever, remained an island of generosity, never too precious with his music and allowing the others to twist and rework his basic chord/melody blocks. All they needed now was one top cover version to complete the eight-song set. Guigsy, tastefully, selected 'No Love Lost' – a Joy Division classic, of course, but the Rain would play it as released on a rare vinyl-only demo,

stripped-down and colder. It was a cool choice, and
certainly a classy step up from 'Wild Thing'. (Some
Oasis books later claimed that the Rain were simply
a cover versions band. They only ever performed two
covers in their career – less than Oasis's tally, to be
pedantic.)

The careful planning had paid off: the band entered
the Times Square to find it packed, with the Rain
T-shirts dotted liberally about the crowd. The lads were
flying now, totally committed to the performance; it
was one of the best gigs the Rain ever did, despite
their inexperience as a unit. For Chris in particular, aware that the band's music was not generic
baggy Madchester but something darker and more
intense, the audience reaction validated everything
he believed. Belonging to a lineage that owed more
to Joy Division, the Bunnymen and the Smiths was
not necessarily going to mean commercial suicide –
'their people' would respond to something more than
funky drummer beats and poppy vocals.

As soon as they came off stage, an effusive bloke
came charging over to them, announcing himself as
the manager of the Midwich Cuckoos. They were a
near-local band, from Stockport, with a much bigger
name than the Rain, yet here was their manager
offering to take the Rain on and give his full commitment to them. The lads knew the guy had some
good connections down at KFM Radio, and the fact
that he'd already taken such an average band as the

Cuckoos so far spoke of some ability. But the band took an instant dislike to him: 'Too fat, and a big mouth.' They declined his offer, sure in the knowledge that something better would turn up. Tonight's success had made them feel they could expect the best from now on.

Maybe, in retrospect, that was one chance blown. Another went west a week later, after the lads staged an almighty piss-up and kitchens-raid at Raffles, culminating in a surreal frozen-fish fight. Stumbling into the bar, they found three Scousers in an even worse state than themselves, slumped over dozens of drained pint-pots. One looked completely unconscious, but the lads recognized him as some big wheel in The Farm machine, the lumbering Liverpudlians who were currently riding the Groovy Train for all it was worth. It went against the grain to ask a Scouser for anything – bar 'the time' outside Old Trafford, of course – but Chris swallowed his Red pride and asked one of the conscious pair if their comatose mate might be able to help out the band. 'Don't bother,' slurred Bazza number one, 'if you wake that fucker up, he'll just want to batter you – he's well out of it.' Chris, barely able to stand himself, withdrew; later, as the Farm basked in their 15 minutes, he wished he'd been more persistent.

For the time being, Bonehead's brother Martin agreed to step in as temporary gaffer until they could find someone permanent. Martin was no pro manager, always happier surrounded by disembowelled recording consoles and patch-boxes, but he had a lot of music-biz contacts and a rough idea of what a new band should be doing. It was a smart decision. Martin pulled out the stops, knowing he was helping his brother to escape the drudgery of the plastering game, and secured them a second, better-paid gig at the Times Square for the end of October. A few calls to the right people secured the Rain some press attention too: the South Manchester press gave the lads a couple of plugs and the *Manchester Evening News* flagged up the gig on their pop page. The Rain had now formally arrived on the scene, and the next audience would not be theirs to select through careful targeting, but unpredictable Joe Public. The band were right to be slightly nervous at the prospect of stepping out from their close social circle.

When they walked into the club on the night of October 31, the change in atmosphere was tangible. The club was crawling with lads they'd never seen: outsiders, pissed-up hoolies and a couple of real 'boys', the latter appearing to be more interested in casing the joint than smoking one. 'Bad vibes, this,' muttered Chris, a moment before the first bottle came sailing through the air, just missing his forehead. From the stage vantage point, the scene resembled a suburban Altamont, as rucking broke out all over the floor. 'This is like the fuckin' terraces at Old Trafford,' shouted Chris, before ordering the band off-stage.

The Rain may not have been as loved-up a band as some in the Madchester vibe, but they weren't

Bonehead, the Shentons
and the Moran brothers in
'Perry Boy'/moustache
embarrassment, *1984*
(© Steve Shenton)

Burnage High School
(© Chris Hutton)

A quick tour around
the lads' manor:
(©Chris Hutton)

Liam and Noel's
(above)

Guigsy's
(below)

Bonehead's
(left)

BURNAGE LANE

Hodge, Bonehead
(with hair)
and Pat Moran
crash the ash
(©John Hodkinson)

Guigsy, Hodge, Tony French and
John Moran tanking up before
the Roses' Paris gig, *1989*
(©John Hodkinson)

Liam aged fourteen
(©Mark Shenton)

Hodge, Tony French, Chris, Bonehead and Dave get their ties out for the lads *(©John Hodkinson)*

Hodge and the squired-up 'Bonemobile' at Spike Island, *1990 (©John Hodkinson)*

Guigsy, Dave, Veronica, Tony French, 'Bully','Griff' and, on the van, Chris with the missus, and Bonehead, Spike Island, *1990 (©John Hodkinson)*

The Garage aka Club 061 where the Oasis sound was born...
(©Chris Hutton)

And The Milestone where the group was formed
(©Chris Hutton)

Pat Moran, Chris, Guigs and Tony French mark the full moon, *York, 1990 (©John Hodkinson)*

The Rain's first public appearance at the Bridge Club, Withington, *1990*
(©Chris Hutton)
(above and below)

Raffles Hotel where Liam cased out the band
(©Chris Hutton)

LOCAL BAND NIGHT FEATURING

THE RAIN

LIVE AT THE BOARDWALK
LITTLE PETER STREET, MANCHESTER

SUNDAY 6th JANUARY

ADVANCE TICKETS £3.00

A fan waits for The Rain in Didsbury, *1990 (©Chris Hutton)*

Guigs, B.J. and Chris's
daughter (named after the
Roses' 'Elizabeth, My Dear'
(©Chris Hutton)

Erwood Park where
Oasis FC plied their trade
(©Chris Hutton)

Oasis Mark 1- left to right:
Liam, Guigsy, Noel,
Tony Mac, Bonehead
(©Paul Slattery/Retna)

the Sex Pistols either. Riots at gigs tend only to be fun for the band when there's twenty bouncers in the pit guaranteeing safety – this was too close for comfort. It was no surprise to the lads, when they returned to the venue next day, that the place had been comprehensively robbed and trashed overnight. The intruders had, however, left every item of the Rain's gear untouched. 'Must've enjoyed our songs,' smiled Chris. Appealing to both Generation E *and* the bootboy firms – that was good going . . .

There had been one moody lad in the audience the band did recognize: Liam Gallagher. You'd know those eyebrows anywhere, despite the fact that Liam had jettisoned all his old homeboy gear and adopted the standard Madchester garb. He never said a word to the band – not that he had the chance to, amidst the mayhem – but Chris noticed the hard stare, rarely leaving him as he prowled around the stage. In fact, it would have been a touch unsettling if Chris hadn't had rather more going on around his head to worry about. What was Liam doing? Staring him out as a prelude to fisticuffs, or studying Chris's 'stagecraft'? The Rain would be seeing more and more of Liam over the next year, a brooding presence at the foot of their stages, taking mental notes.

A couple of weeks after the riot, Martin Arthurs came up trumps yet again. He'd secured the band two five-hour recording session slots at Out of the Blue in town, dirt cheap because he'd done them a couple of desks in the past. Anyone who's ever been in a band knows how the old first-studio-session two-step goes: intense excitement and anticipation, followed by tedium and disappointment. And so it was for the Rain. Guigs, Tony and Chris had never been inside a studio before and were buzzing all Friday night – only Bonehead, who'd done a session with Pleasure In Pain, knew what awaited and remained blasé.

As Chris got up on Saturday morning, he groaned with the realization that he was getting flu; hardly an auspicious start. Then there was the nagging doubt that they'd chosen the wrong songs to do – 'All of You', 'Blues of Youth', 'Kinetic' – and the nerve-wrecking wait for the engineer to turn up (no demo session in world history ever started on time, though your studio bill never seems to reflect that).

Once inside, it's never as glamorous as you thought it'd be: too many rock videos have filled your head with flying faders, enormous sound rooms and monster effects banks. Generally, you've done well to get an old eight-track, a broken wah-wah pedal and a mike covered in some tart's smelly nylons. And nothing can prepare you for the endless level-testings, mike set-ups and tedious, passion-killing repetition (nothing is more soul-destroying than the phrase 'Vocal track, take twenty-two'.) Nor are you ready for the cruel exposure of your fluffs and minor tremors as the Ampex replays your solo performance, those rough-diamond edges which give the reality to your gig sound but reverberate mockingly in the dead air of a studio. For anyone who wants simply to be in a band, rather than be a 'recording artiste', the verdict on a first session is always as Chris's was that weekend: 'Boring, monotonous and very disappointing.' Oh, not forgetting the final golden rule of the demo session: however long you've booked in for, it's never enough to finish what you'd planned. The Rain had to junk their most famous song, 'Rooftop Rave', half-done in order to have time for mix-down. (This is the point where you all gang up and recriminate with the drummer about the half-hour it took him to tune up his toms.)

Still: they had a tape, something to push and plug. It would have to do for now, so the boys resolved to be positive. After all, no band ever produced a top-notch first demo; indeed, most try to have any tapes burned or buried as soon as they hit the big time. You try getting hold of the first dodgy Oasis demo, for example.

Tony Wilson, as you'd expect, certainly knew all about first-demo syndrome. When the lads pulled themselves together, they went looking for the Factory supremo's house, Bonehead declaring that he'd refuse to leave until Wilson took the tape. Chris knew what street Wilson lived on whereas Bonehead claimed he'd recognize his car which he'd seen outside the Haç; the detective work succeeded. Guigs refused to go to the door so the other two strode forward. A paranoid-looking Wilson opened the door gingerly, his missus peeping around the lounge door. (Chris whispered to Bonehead, 'Is he on something? Or does he think we're gonna rob his house?') Bonehead blundered on with it: 'We're the Rain. Here's our demo – listen to it and sign us up to Factory.' Bluntly Burnage, as ever.

Wilson, recovering somewhat, barked back: 'I don't listen to demo-tapes. Send it to Phil at A&R.' Bonehead's protests that he didn't want to end up at the bottom of an unheard pile were futile; Wilson shut the door in his face. He probably had better things to do, like preside over a bankruptcy and foist Northside upon us. It wouldn't be the last time he'd let a Bonehead band slip through his clutches either. It won't look good in the obits will it? 'The Man Who Failed to Sign Oasis – Twice'. But preferable to 'He Thought "Take Five" Was A Classic'.

'Fuck 'im – let's get pissed' concluded the boys, turning away from the house. That night, they rallied around each other, drinking to the future, dreaming the dream. In a stupor, they each made a solemn promise to each other for the coming New Year. Guigs: 'I am not going to become a fat bastard, right? No more chips, I mean it, slap me if you see me on the chips – and I'm going weight training every week. Promise.' Tony Mac: 'All right, I'll stop playing the Mick, just lay off with the plastic Paddy shit.' Bonehead: 'I'm gonna save me hair. I'm not going to be a slaphead. If I rub my fingernails together every hour like this, I've heard it stops your hair falling out.' (Eh?!)

Chris: 'Right, if you lot do that, I promise to read a book all the way through for the first time in my life.' (And as a slightly more concrete token of their band-bonding, Chris lent Tony Mac £250 which he'd saved from his factory wages to sort out the crumbling drum kit.)

They rounded the night off with a party-planning session. Christmas with the Rain would mean taking over the top floor of Squires in Didsbury, getting Rosy in on the decks and organizing a support band which the Rain would follow. Reluctance, the band they'd shared the Green Room with, were up for it. The lads ended up printing proper tickets and getting bar extensions sorted, such was the local demand to be there. The band were beginning to grasp that they were local names now, 'faces' to be let onto in the street – their Xmas do was the hot ticket of the seasonal period. (Chris still laughs at the memory of three local girls, rushing up to him at a bus-stop, squealing: 'Ooh, aren't you that fit singer out of the Rain?')

So despite the Wilson knock-back and the disappointment of the demo session, Christmas found the Rain on top, buzzing and ready to make it in '91. They believed in themselves – and the 250 sell-out gig at Squires confirmed they had fellow believers. Chris remembers it as the best gig they ever played. It was time for the Rain to leave the suburbs, head into the city and prove themselves to the world.

Bonehead, getting cockier by the day, marched down to The Boardwalk in town with the demo tape as soon as Christmas was over. And this time he really wasn't leaving until they gave him an answer. The Boardwalk was a name venue, on the proper circuit, the sort of place the *NME* turned up at. Moreover, its reputation was built on breaking new local acts, sucking in bands from outside the city centre to try their luck in front of a knowing metropolitan audience. Bonehead had his eye on the next Band Night, where three or four local acts would showcase themselves, hoping to sell the most tickets to get headline status. Getting on the bill guaranteed a plug in the *Evening News*, maybe a namecheck or two on Piccadilly Radio, and the chance to be spotted by the A&R and promoter types who lurked in the venue's recesses. It was the kind of place no music-biz pro or fan could afford to take their eye off lest they missed the next big thing, since every major Manchester band had played here early on.

Bonehead, whose impressive presence tended to guarantee acquiescence from all but those of Tony Wilson status, succeeded. They liked the tape and promised the Rain a slot for the night of January 6. In just eight months, Chris had led his band from conception to the brink of industry recognition – yet within four more, it would all be over.

11

The Queen is Dead

Before the Rain's second gig, Chris had insisted that the band should always appear with one essential stage prop, an item which would transmit the band's sense of identity and belonging to the audience: the British flag. At the time, there was no less cool or more suspect symbol to utilize in such a way. The reigning pop ideology of 1991–2 posited that waving the flag was racist, pure and simple. There was no room for irony, nor for any notion of 'reclaiming' the nation's colours, as the débâcle of Finsbury Park in '92 would demonstrate. Chris knew something of this mindset but ignored it. He still believed that patriotic sentiment and a pride in one's roots should be accepted rather than immediately deemed crypto-fascist. By adopting such a stance, the Rain possibly risked the sort of conclusion-jumping that blighted Joy Division's reputation, but they never appeared without the flag again as photos from the time prove.

Now, five years later, Chris watches with amusement as the trend he started has become epidemic. The symbol of British popular music and culture in 1997 is the Union Jack. Whether it be on Noel's guitar, Geri Spice's dress, Liam 'n' Patsy's cover-shoots or Bowie's McQueen jacket, the flag has been prominently reclaimed by our country's most famous faces. But it was Oasis who spearheaded the trend, resurrecting Chris's original concept though with less clearly defined objectives.

For the use of the flag remains mired in ambivalence, the symbol still being one that divides, that can speak for quite different agendas. Bowie's use is surely ironic, Geri's politically suspect and Oasis's simply baffling, given their leader's contradictory attitudes towards his identity and roots. The very concept of the flag speaks of the strangeness inherent in our constitution and identity. What is the United Kingdom and Britishness anyway? The flag and the definitions of identity surrounding it are riddled with confusion. Only in that sense, as we shall see, does it become an appropriate symbol for Oasis to use.

Ironically, Chris didn't want the Union Jack to start with anyway. What he really wanted was an English flag of St George, for he defined himself as Mancunian and *English* above all else. But before Euro '96, such flags were hard to come by; English nationalism was always taken to imply British nationalism. Declaring oneself English first and foremost was both honest and sensitive, as well as free from the baggage of

British-ism. Now, as the combination of devolution and the EU philosophy of a Europe of regions takes hold, this point of view seems more apt than ever. The joke on the Union Jack brigade is that 'Britain' and 'Britishness' have never seemed less relevant than they do today.

The only greater loyalty Chris felt than that which he owed to England was to Manchester. When tattooing became the craze of the week one Burnage summer, Chris chose a simple design which he continues to bear with pride: 'MUFC' on the cross of St George. It's almost like a manufacturer's stamp on him. A popular chant at Old Trafford was always 'Born and bred in Manchester', a tribal allegiance and cultural inheritance which many locals place above those of nationhood. This belief can work for everyone born and bred in this city: those from immigrant cultures or of different ethnicities call themselves Mancunian and are generally accepted as such. You don't have to be white or 'pure English' to be a Manc, something which cannot always be said for other cities.

The Rain were always determined to reflect their roots, especially in the raw material of their songs. Singing about Strangeways, Burnage High schooldays, a specifically Mancunian urban teenage existence and so forth gave their Manc-ness an 'in-yer-face' quality which they liked and cultivated. If they could have a more universal resonance, so be it; but they would not seek to downplay their origins or remove their geographical references in order to gain that. One feature they always adored in their heroes was their blatant local identity. The moment you heard his voice, you knew where Morrissey was coming from; and Joy Division's music seemed inextricably bound up with the dark architecture and drizzling atmosphere of the late seventies Manchester city centre.

Sadly, what one might term regional or urban patriotism became as politically incorrect later in the eighties as the more bigoted '-isms'. Bands such as the Stone Roses, despite benefiting in popularity because of the coolness associated with being Mancunian, eschewed parochial sentiment in favour of a floating universality, which resulted in Ian Brown's famed 'It's not where you're from . . .' aphorism. At the Paris Roses gig in '89, John Squire was heard to express embarrassment about the chants of 'Manchester la la la' from the imported audience, a rare example of the band's attitudes being out of kilter with the fans'. Cynics suggest that bands often make such noises in order not to alienate potential record-buyers outside their hometowns, although this was never alleged in relation to such a blatantly uncalculating band as the Roses.

Noel's use of the flag and attitudes to England and Manchester are ambiguous. In Hewitt's book, it is claimed that the band's interest in the flag came from The Who's example, not mentioning the very different motivation behind the Rain's. Moreover, the Who's intentions were obvious and bound up with their Pop Art manifesto, whereas Oasis's ideology is far less discernible. Noel's explanation of the thinking behind the key song 'Red White And Blue' (not released at the time of writing), is similarly confusing. The lyrics apparently tackle questions about identity and unwelcome pigeon-holing, yet Noel's comments only succeed in muddying the waters, especially when he adds that playing the song on record would cause more trouble than it's worth. What does the flag signify? Is it some sort of ironic piss-take, an attempt to reclaim it from abusive manipulation, an attempt to portray themselves as a Brit band for Brits? Does Noel really know why, or is it another product of the muddled thinking that passes for Oasis's mission statement, with its vague talk of freedom and escape?

It would appear that there is a simultaneous embracing and rejection of British values going on here. The issue is further complicated by Noel's approach to his Irish inheritance. A troubled childhood with his monstrous father seems to have perverted the relationship with his Irish roots. Throughout his adolescence, he rejected 'plastic Paddyism' and avoided Irish influences, yet in recent years he has made much of his ancestry and played up the imprint left upon his compositions by Irish folk and bands like the Wolftones. Does this mean he is now proud to be recognized as, predominantly, an Irishman? If so, what does his use of the flag signify? If he rejects such talk of national and ethnic identity and prefers to see himself as a rootless, existentialist individual, why draw any attention whatsoever to these issues in the first place by flaunting the flag and allying oneself with the Britmod pack?

Noel's view of Manchester is also hard to pin down. In an early *NME* interview, he growled, 'That city's done us no favours, man', which, coupled with some onstage criticism of lads chanting 'Manchester la la la', created an impression of weak allegiance to the city. Leaving town to live in London isn't a crime – Morrissey, for one, got away with it – but his prompt exit in late '93 irritated some faithful locals. The band's reluctance to stay in touch with their roots and the controversy over the lack of generosity in their Maine Road 'Thank you' gigs maintained the sense of betrayal some felt. The band were obviously not inspired by the example of New Order, who not only stayed around the city but ploughed money back into it via the Haç and the *Dry 201* bar. Even the one enduring Mancunianism about them, their very public support for Man City FC, convinces less than you'd expect. Some Maine Road regulars mutter about their non-attendance at matches and their supposed showboating when they do turn up. To many Blues, they were behaving like their caricature of the hated Reds as flash-harry part-timers. Indeed, it has been suggested that the relentless promotion of their City allegiance is clever marketing to a nation that hates Man United rather than a long-standing fascination.

Overall, Oasis have managed to generate as much suspicion as adoration within the city that spawned them. They may have sold more records than any Manchester greats of the past but they have yet to become as cherished as New Order or the Stone Roses and probably never will be. Some of that, admittedly, is part of the syndrome that expels those who become too popular and successful from the hometown's bosom – a tendency which has left Simply Red's Mick Hucknall on many a Mancunian's most-hated list. But primarily, it is not a question of envy or 'selling-out', rather a reflection on the lack of initial emotional connection between the band and city. They don't mean as much to each other as they should.

In defence of Noel, there seems to be good reason for some of this. He was an unhappy kid and not exactly an ecstatic teenager, living in an atmosphere of abuse and relative poverty. Manchester will forever conjure up memories of that existence. If his songs stand for anything, they stand for escapist liberation, and for relying upon concentrated individual strength to break the strait-jacket of one's environment. Inevitably, Manchester must seem to be part of that which he sought to flee and transcend. Perhaps, as he did with his Irish ancestry, he will eventually come to a happier accommodation with Manchester when he is fully able to appreciate what it gave him and not just how it might have hurt him.

12

This Night Has Opened My Eyes

When the Rain turned up at The Boardwalk to soundcheck on the 6th, they realized they'd stepped up in the world. Who was that guy out on the floor waiting for them? A sound engineer . . . with a top-notch mixing desk . . . who appeared to care about how they'd sound . . . which they could hear through proper stage monitors, at last. Sorted! So this was professionalism – it beat getting a mate to frantically twiddle amp controls between numbers up on the Times Square stage. And welcome also to the world of pro spin-doctoring and manipulation. The Rain hadn't 'won' the headline spot, which didn't bother them too much, but they then were amazed to see that the crowd overwhelmingly consisted of their own supporters. A world-weary staffer explained the deal to Chris: the 'headliners' had bought their own tickets in bulk just to secure top spot. That meant first billing in the press and that they could honestly claim to have 'headlined the Boardwalk' on their next press release. 'Pathetic

yet cunning, like all good PR.' The Rain blew them
off stage anyway: Chris's intensity and Bonehead's
arena-soaking roar made up for any lack of finesse.

Watching from the front again was Liam Gallagher,
all studied concentration and brow-heavy glower. The
band expected him to be there now – ever since the
Didsbury riot, Liam had taken to coming down to
Raffles for the Rain's rehearsals, where he'd mooch
about the cellars, listen carefully to their developing
songs and watch Chris practising his technique and
moves. He never said much, at least not to Chris,
but after the first couple of visits the band got used
to having him around. Privately, Chris would laugh
at Liam's cling-on status: what exactly was he doing
there anyway? He and Liam had never got on; the guy
never talked to Chris about the Rain's music and he
was the wrong sex to be a groupie. Still, once or twice
Chris would come back from the bar and find Liam
had cornered Guigsy or Bonehead – what were they
talking about? The lads would shrug noncommittally.
Only much later, when it was too late, did Chris guess
what Liam had been up to.

Elsewhere in the Boardwalk crowd was reputed to be
the Happy Mondays' Shaun Ryder, whom the boys had
met at an ACR gig the previous week, and an increasingly
interested Andy Rourke. The lads knew they had to
strike now, while the white-out noise of their finale was
still ringing in the ears. To get any further, they needed
a full-time manager – Martin wouldn't be around for
much longer. Chris hared round to Rourke's house and

laid his cards on the table. The Rain wanted to give their full commitment; they knew they had something going here. If Rourke told them not to bother, they'd take it on the chin – but if he thought they had a chance, they needed his help. Rourke didn't hesitate: 'Here's my home phone number, Chris: give me a ring the day after tomorrow and I'll see what I can do for you.'

Forty-eight hours on tenterhooks ended in relief. Guigs phoned Rourke back, who invited the band round to his house. Did they want the good news or the good news? First up, he'd found them an agent, a guy who'd worked for the Smiths for years. He'd told him the score and he was keen to get involved. Secondly, how did the lads fancy doing a real demo, of near-releasable quality, at Rourke's own home studio? They'd have all the time they needed to get it bang-on, and Rourke himself would produce it as well as allow the band to drop his name wherever necessary when promoting it. The lads managed to stop grinning long enough to say 'Yes please'.

Guigs, being smart and a good talker, was deputed to talk to the agent Rourke had recommended. A week later, Chris met Guigs at The Tivoli in Longsight for the debriefing. 'Well, what's happening?' Chris demanded. 'We're gonna be pop stars,' hooted Guigsy. 'He says get the demo done, and a home vid of us playing, and he'll sort us out.' At Raffles, the band decided to put everything they had into just one song for the demo – they were in too good a position now to fuck up by over-extending themselves. It had to make a definitive statement about the band: they needed something a touch darker than their earlier rabble-rousing gear, a song that meant something to both writer and listener, in a style that illustrated the lineage to which they belonged.

They chose 'Black', one of their slowest and heaviest pieces but one which demonstrated Bonehead's grasp of classic rock structure and pacing. Above all, it had a lyric, largely penned by Guigsy, which was a world away from the E'd up nonsense that was the day's common currency. Guigs had written it at 16, at his most confused, insecure and even suicidal; the debt to Curtis and Morrissey was obvious but the emotion expressed was clearly personal, not adopted. The contrast with their contemporaries was striking as the South sunk into the blank vapidities of shoegazing whilst the North indulged in the hedonism of the Mondays' *Pills 'n' Thrills and Bellyaches* and *Penthouse* editorship. The Rain were, perhaps, ahead of their time: a year later, when Nirvana began their conquest of Britain, their spirit might have been more in tune with the zeitgeist.

Five days before they were due to record the demo, a slice of Guigsy naughtiness caught up with him and the band. The Raffles manageress, with whom Guigsy had boasted of sleeping, had been alerted to his claims. After making it quite clear that her standards could never have fallen so low as to accommodate pallid bass players, she turfed them out of the cellars for good. The lads were too busy taking the piss out of the blushing Guigsy to ruminate on their loss of facilities.

The demo session went sweetly – except for poor Tony Mac, who couldn't do his drum part because there wasn't room for the kit. Samples and loops serviced as a replacement. Bonehead added some keyboards, as the band were plotting to become a five-piece, with his old mate John Moran coming in for gigs as ivory-tinkler. The band also discussed adding a lead guitarist – Chris suggested Noel Gallagher. 'I'll go and get his demo tape and we'll decide off that.' The band's verdict? 'Nah, it's shit.' Chris erased the tape and with it disappeared an historic opportunity . . . and about £100,000 resale value. The second they'd run off a copy from the mixed DAT, the band raced round to the place in Fallowfield Bonehead was sharing with his wife-to-be Kate. Endless rounds of drinks, endless rewinds and replays: this was the dog's bollocks, at last. Something to be proud of, something which truly stated what they were and believed in. All four were euphoric.

But the song, as Chris remarked, was truly 'double sad'. We can't reprint the lyric verbatim because Guigsy has copyright but it spoke graphically of the blackness at the heart of his teenage life. The band hoped it also spoke to those thousands of Manc lads who've recognized a similar void in their adolescences. Guigsy wrote about abject anonymity, the inability to express emotion, the traumatic after-effects of his first drug-use (calling cannabis 'the seed of hate'), the directionlessness of suburban existence and even of suicide's appeal. Chris and the Rain had offered him an escape from that existential crisis. It doesn't do him much credit that he apparently now seeks to denigrate those who helped him to succeed.

Quite rightly, their agent was encouraging. He felt they could do business now but had one suggestion to make: could they change the name? The Scouse guitar band Rain hadn't complained but the possibilities of confusion were obvious. Terry Christian, when he plugged their initial Boardwalk gig in the *Manchester Evening News*, had made the same mistake, dubbing Chris's outfit 'Rain' and warning readers not to mistake Scousers for Mancs. The lads weren't happy with the idea. The Rain perfectly summed them up and, despite hours of brain-storming, they couldn't come up with another they liked. They proposed a compromise: in tribute to the Roses, they'd go for Cinnamon Rain. But within days, they sacked it. 'Let the Scousers take us on,' argued Chris. 'Soon, it'll be them who'll have to change their name, not us.'

And his confidence seemed justified as, within the week, 'Black' received its first airplay on KFM Radio in Manchester. The DJ gave the band a good plug, pointed his listeners in the direction of their next Boardwalk gig on April 15, then immediately played a Smiths single. The four lads, all time-served Smiths devotees, basked in the moment. They had a Smiths producer, the Smiths' agent and now were deemed worthy to stand side-by-side with a Morrissey–Marr classic on their favourite radio station. Chris marvelled at the reality: they were now seemingly entering the sunlit uplands where the dreams he and Guigsy had shared throughout their teenage years were starting to come true. In fact, Chris's nightmare was almost upon him.

There didn't seem to be a cloud in the Rain's sky. The other three never seemed anything but happy, committed and close. Certainly, Bone and Guigs had never before had such an opportunity to express themselves artistically and appeared to be relishing it. The sole deviation from their united approach had come from Bonehead, who wanted the band to steer clear from becoming too doom-laden and Joy Division-influenced. No problem: they all loved the Roses, so a few Bonehead jangles would be fine to lighten the pace and mood. Above all, no one had ever questioned Chris's singing or performances. Guigsy in particular had only ever encouraged and enthused – whenever he had constructive criticism to offer, Chris would take it. And all three original members had input into the writing, so there could be no cause for song-credit wrangles. As a band built upon friendship and completely shared influences, with no visible fault-lines, Chris felt assured that nothing could bring them down. Especially as the core relationship, which gave the band its ideology and sense of purpose, was the one between him and Guigs. Best mates. Loyal. United.

April 15, 1991: Chris simply never felt better. Man United had just scored a brilliant triumph in Poland, virtually securing a place in the European Cup Winners' Cup Final. All those years scrimping and jibbing with the Reds during the darker seasons were about to be amply rewarded. Domestic life was sweet: a beautiful missus and a healthy, happy baby daughter with the promise of a better financial life around the corner. And the Rain appeared set up for the final push towards a deal and a career, headlining at the Boardwalk with plans made for a mini-album demo.

It was soundcheck time: Tony Mac hadn't made it yet, still stuck down a hole in a Levenshulme road, but they'd borrowed the support band's drummer for their run-through. Guigsy perked up as his favourite was due – 'No Love Lost'. A couple of months back, he'd bumped into one of his heroes, Hooky (Peter Hook, bassist of Joy Division and New Order), and told him proudly that they did a mint version of it as their star turn. Hooky looked pleased – leaving Guigsy buzzing. As they finished their performance, the sound mixer came to the front of the stage. Someone said that he'd done gigs with New Order and Joy Division in the past; he appeared quite moved. It was a most un-Mancunian moment. 'I just wanna say, you lads did proper justice to that. That was pure quality.' Chris beamed – this is what it's all about. An emotional connection. A sense of spirit.

Chris used to have piles of tapes of the Rain's music: the studio demos, of course, and stacks of rehearsal sessions over which the band would pore, looking for riffs and snatches of improvisation that really worked. But not one ever captured the band at its best – live, in front of an audience, on top form. All he keeps now is a fragment from this last gig, both as memento and as proof that they gelled as a live band. Listening to it, he is transported back – to a 'mad for it' youth, to the era of baggy shuffles and T-shirts, to a time when he thought the world would be theirs.

It's notoriously difficult to describe how a band sounds in print. If you pigeon-holed the Rain as a cross between Joy Division and baggy, that might help; but it would be better if you had a copy of the Oasis/Real People demo, as many hardcore fans do. Imagine 'Take Me', but harder and faster; remove Liam's more conventional singing and replace with the declamatory style Chris favoured, more Shaun Ryder than Ian Brown. Chuck in some rather more specific lyrics, turn up Bonehead's distortion and that would be close enough to suffice. Strangely, given the Rain's non-commercial approach, most of Bonehead's songs for them had rather more pronounced choruses than 'Take Me' – indeed, 'Rooftop Rave' and 'All of You' were shamelessly catchy. (Intriguingly, 'All of You' boasts a musical chorus almost identical to those in 'Rock 'n' Roll Star' and 'Shakermaker', giving weight to speculation about Bonehead's under-reported musical input into Oasis.)

The band are into their last ten minutes and are beginning to steam. Tony Mac is shuffling like a madman now, combining classic baggy beats with Steve Morris rolls and patterns, completely tight with Guigsy's rudimentary bass. Bonehead's guitar, dare we admit it, has a touch of Northside effect on it, sweeping jangles across 'All of You', before Chris announces 'Closer', their tribute to Ian Curtis. He's building himself up now to the climax, letting loose trademark Madchester yelps and howls in best Ryder fashion. Bonehead, thankfully, lays off the Northsidery and starts Who-style power-chording through the throbbing finale of 'Closer', inducing Tony Mac into massive bass drum double-detonations. Chris pauses and announces 'A year ago, it was kicking off round the corner', before launching into 'Rooftop Rave'. His singing in the chorus is manic, celebratory, yelling Paul Taylor's name at the crowd lest they miss the point. In the coda, he's almost taking the piss out of pop, crooning the 'ba-ba-bas' like a West Coast popster, totally at odds with the context.

As the band crash to a close, there's a second's pause, not much more than the drop-out in 'Resurrection' – which is deliberate, for their closing number seeks the same wigged-out intensity as their favourite Roses song. Chris shouts '*Acid Rain Dance*' and then he's off, 'into one'. He doesn't sing a word but loses himself in the music, which is perhaps the best of the night. A combination of mad sixties spy-film riffery and full-on Madchester rhythm, it features Guigs with an uncharacteristically complex bass-line (painstakingly taught to him by Bonehead, and flawlessly executed) and some superb Bone lead guitar, backed by Tony Mac at his most thunderous. The dynamics and inter-play are spot on, the understanding compelling, as the music swells into crescendo. A brief, white-out burst and it's over. Chris grins: now *that* was the business. As he hollers good night to the crowd, he can have no idea that he'll never address an audience again.

As they came off stage, Chris looked round for his mate Guigs, ready to go off for a drinks session. Over in a corner, he could see Guigs and Liam, seemingly in urgent conversation. They looked somehow foreign to him, conspiratorial even. He headed for the bar.

Eventually, Guigs showed up for a bottle or two. 'All right, Paul?' inquired Chris. For a second, Guigs looked blankly, coldly, straight through him. Like he wasn't there. Like he'd never existed. Guigs muttered something, looking down at the floor. Chris had been with Guigs through too many mood-swings and depressions in his life not to know when to back off. But there was something in Guigsy's stone-hard expression that was new to him. The bar felt colder now. Chris went home.

The following night, Chris mooched about his house, flicking listlessly through his records, waiting for Guigs to show up. He'd always come round, have a beer, review the gig; in fact, he was round most nights anyway. Strange that he'd not turned up. Stranger still that he didn't show the following night either. 'Perhaps I should phone? Nah, don't be soft: what are you, married or summat?' Besides, there was no phone in the house – silly to go trekking off down the road to the phonebox for nothing. Unless there was something to be concerned about. Which there wasn't, right?

Next day, on his way to the offie, Chris spotted

Bonehead driving down Kingsway. He pulled over as soon as he saw Chris. 'All right mate; what's going on, then?' asked Chris as casually as he could. Bonehead shrugged: 'Not much we can do is there, now we're out of them rehearsal rooms? Me and Guigs have been jamming a bit round my place. We're putting it on tape for you so you can do some words and that. Give you a bell when it's sorted, yeah?'

Fair enough, thought Chris: they'd all agreed to see if Bonehead could knock up something more Roses-like, so best to let him get on with it. Didn't explain why Guigs was keeping so fucking quiet though, did it?

Another 48 hours passed. Enough's enough. Chris lurched down to the phonebox to call Guigsy.

'All right, Paul?'

'All right.'

'So . . . what's happening then?'

'What d'yer mean?'

'Well, the band, everything. You've not been round my place, y'know . . . what about the band rehearsing an' that?'

A slight pause. Then, Guigsy, cool as fuck: 'The band? I think we're splittin' up.'

It's always an achievement not to drop the handset at such a moment. Complete head-fuck. Not really takin' this in, mate.

'What? What? What d'you mean "we're splittin' up"?'

And while Chris's head is in pieces – trying to make

sense of what he's been told, reassuring himself that it can't be right, everything's going so well, the Rain was on its way – Guigs is gliding smoothly along, the result of some lengthy blarney-preparation: 'Yeah, that agent says this isn't gonna work out unless we're all hundred per cent, like on the dole and ready to tour the country full-time . . .'

'All right, all right,' interjects Chris, stabbing the air fast with his words, 'we'll do it, I'll sack the job, we'll get it together full-time, c'mon Guigs . . .'

'Leave it – you can't do it, you're gettin' a mortgage,' shot back Guigs, suspiciously quick to dismiss the possibility. Chris was getting steamed now. His head was spinning, he had that draining feeling at the pit of his stomach but he knew none of this was right. It just wasn't on the level.

'Right, so what are you lot gonna do then, are you just sacking music forever or what?' demanded Chris, scepticism apparent in his voice.

Too evenly, Guigs recited: 'I'm gonna learn the bass properly, Tony's joining an Irish folk band and Bonehead needs to earn some money – Martin repossessed his guitar.'

'Come on, Guigsy, this is mad, we've all gotta sit down and discuss this, you can't just do one like this.'

'I gotta go, Chris. I'm off training. I've not got time to discuss this.'

'Right then. I'm getting off.'

'Right then.'

Chris replaced the receiver, turned back down the road and looked into a blank, dream-less future.

What could he tell his missus? How do you explain the end of something you'd put a year of your life into when you don't have any reason you can believe yourself? She told him to get round to Bonehead's and have it out. Maybe his version would be more convincing.

As he stalked down the roads towards Bonehead's house, his mind felt like it was burning, in turmoil. What could have gone wrong? How could such a solid structure collapse in an instant like that? How could Guigsy just give up without a fight? He turned into Bonehead's road, then froze. There, outside the driveway, was Guigsy's car. No time to talk about the end of a dream with his best mate but apparently time enough to be at Bonehead's. He felt the first icy slivers of impending doom, the feeling every suspicious husband or outmanoeuvred business partner knows, the shiver you get just before you're faced with the proof of abandonment.

Kate answered the door, surprised by the identity of the visitor. Chris headed for the back room, scene of many a band session. As he stood in the doorway, two familiar blushing faces looked up at him – Guigs and Bonehead. An awful pause, stomach-tightening and intense.

'I thought you were going training, Paul,' remarked Chris softly.

'I've, ah, come to tell Bone the score first, y'know . . .' Guigsy's voice trailed off.

'All right then. All right. What is the score? Have we split up – and why?'

Guigs pulls himself together: 'Look, it's like I said. We're all off to do our own thing, right? I told you.'

Chris couldn't find any more words for now. This situation had done his head in. All he could manage to stutter was, 'Right . . . fair enough.' Which of course, it wasn't. It was probably the least appropriate remark he'd made since telling everyone United would win the league in '89. Another churning silence fell upon the three, full of unexpressed emotions and vital words left unsaid. Bonehead flicked the tape deck on. The intro to 'Black' filled the room. No one spoke.

Guigs and Chris shuffled out of the house, neither looking the other in the eye. 'I really do have to go to training,' mumbled Guigs. 'I'll probably see you at the weekend, Chris.' And with that, he drove off, to a different and glorious future.

As it happened, Chris barely caught sight of Guigs or Bonehead for the next month or so. Chris wasn't hiding away or anything; why should he? But his comrades seemed to be keeping a low profile, to say the least. He certainly wasn't going to start phoning them up like some pining schoolie; in fact, even though they had not exchanged a word about the state of their friendship, Chris already felt that Guigs was no longer the kind of mate he could just phone for a natter. He still had no proof that anything out of order was happening – but that pit-of-the-stomach feeling recurred almost daily.

At least the grisly tidings came from another mate, not from some piss-taker in the street. Chris had met up with Hodge, a good lad and longstanding pal who'd been at Spike Island with him, and the pair took a stroll through Levenshulme. Hodge had no intention of keeping Chris in the dark: 'Have you heard what Guigsy's up to? He's started to do some work with Liam.'

Chris stopped in his tracks: 'What d'you mean, "work"?'

'Y'know, music an' that. Liam fancies himself as a singer. And I think Bonehead's in on it too.'

Another head-fuck; another hour of spinning turmoil. If this was true . . . his own best mate . . . behind his back . . . bastards, bastards . . . gotta check it out, *now*. Instead of phoning Guigs and getting into God knows what kind of confrontation, he phoned Andy Rourke. If they'd been up to anything, perhaps they'd told Rourke some time over the last few weeks?

'All right, Chris: what's happening? Have you seen the others?'

'Well, no, not for a month now, that's why I'm phoning really.'

'Look, that bass player – Paul, isn't it? – he was round here with your tape and some geek he said was the new singer.'

'What? What did he say?'

'He actually asked me if I could put this new guy's voice over yours on the demo-tape.'

'Jesus. When was this?'

'Must have been at least, what, a month ago.'

A month ago? Bet it was the day after the last Boardwalk gig. Chris listened speechless as Andy went on: 'Anyway, I thought it was out of order. I just told him that if he was gonna be like that, I didn't want any part of it.'

Chris managed to splutter some words of thanks for everything Rourke had done, and for the personal support he'd given him. So his gut feeling had been right. He went home, got his missus, and went out to get royally pissed. This was, after all, a better reason than most to pursue alcoholic obliteration.

Barely had they got started, however, when they ran headlong into Bonehead and Kate at the S&K's bar. Chris composed himself, determined to keep his cool. Public dignity mattered to him; whatever was going on behind closed doors, he had a face and reputation around town to preserve. His missus manoeuvred Kate away so that the lads could talk.

'So what's all this shit I keep hearing, Bonehead: you, Guigs and Liam together an' all that? What's the score?'

'Look Chris, I've got nothin' to do with this. All I know is that Liam got to Guigs after that gig and asked him if he wanted to work together and Guigs said yes.'

'And are you in on it or not?'

'The only thing I've done is that about two weeks later, Guigs asked me to lay down a guitar riff for them, as a favour to a mate. That's all. I'm not in on it.'

'All right. So why don't we do something together, then?'

'Yeah, OK Chris. But I want to change the kind of music we were doing. I'm buzzin' off REM now and I want to get a bit of that into it.'

'Right, no probs. When are we gonna start?'

'Come round my place tomorrow night if you want.'

Chris wanted to give him the benefit of the doubt. Actually, he wanted to do the same for Guigsy. He still couldn't quite believe what he'd done – but the evidence was there to see. Still, Bonehead seemed on-side. At least until he went round the next night, to be told by Kate that Bone was out. *Et tu . . .?*

Once again, poor Hodge had to break the worst to Chris. About a week later, he told Chris he'd been at Bonehead's and had heard a new demo-tape. It sounded very much like a Mancunian REM. The cassette cover told its own story: 'The Rain 1991, featuring Paul Arthurs, Paul McGuigan and Liam Gallagher on vocals'. No shock this time; just a cold, nauseating sense of complete betrayal.

He's a very English guy, Chris. Not for him any rampant histrionics or having it out in the street like a Gallagher. Nor was he going to become a wounded recluse, which would probably have been Guigsy's response to an equivalent calamity. He'd keep his head up around town, carry on living his life, going down the pub. He accepted an invite to a mate's birthday party at the end of the month at the Milestone, knowing that there was a good chance Guigs and Bonehead would be in attendance. He wasn't going to impose social exclusion on himself: he'd done nothing wrong. Sure enough, his ex-bandmates were there. Bonehead was all breezy insouciance, his usual larger-than-life self, taking all the ructions in his stride. But Guigsy was evasive, coy and slightly nervy; he and Chris didn't exchange a word for hours. Only in England! Hours of pot-sinking later, the two somehow found themselves alone in the street, heading for home. Chris broke the painfully awkward silence:

'What's been going on, Paul?'

'What do you mean?'

'Look, don't give me any of that bollocks. I'm not thick, I know what's been happening.'

Guigs kept utterly silent, staring at some convenient fixed point in the distance.

'Well? Are you gonna say anything or what?'

No, he wasn't. Twelve pints inside Chris worked their tongue-loosening magic. For ten minutes, Chris let out everything, all the anger, hurt and resentment. An observer might have feared that at any moment during this onslaught, Chris would simply succumb to his rage and batter several shades out of the bloke. But that wasn't his style – what he wanted was a reaction, a connection. None came. If Guigs felt any guilt it went completely unexpressed. He took it all in silence. Spleen vented and energy drained, Chris went home. It would be six months before they even spoke again.

13

Louder Than Bombs

Happy Mondays by John Robb

Now the dust has cleared: the drugs that we once took for fun have been replaced by nasty habits, the Es that once gave the sweet, sweet rush by mean-spirited smack habits. The free-for-all pills 'n' powder parties that once spilled out over the streets have become grim stand-offs with bitter dealers clutching a fistful of paracetamol and a pocketful of ketamine. Shaun Ryder has moved on from Happy Mondays to the, in many ways far superior, band, Black Grape. We can look back and wonder at that series of madcap parties that the north Mancs outfit threw for us in the back end of the eighties.

The eighties, Christ, the eighties. The filthiest pop decade in history, the most boring, banal, starched-collar pop decade in memory; charts stuffed full of vile mummy's boys and their fluffy-haired bands. It took a small pill called Ecstasy to change this dull state of affairs. (OK, maybe acid first, but you get the drift.)

The Happy Mondays had been around for years. They were a loose gang of mates jamming away in sheds in grey Manchester. The bulk of the band were from the wilderness of Little Hulton – a forgotten council estate in the far north of the city.

Fooling around at school, scamming, making money and falling out the other end, the Ryder brothers became postmen like their dad. Despite its early hours the job had advantages: you could dress like you wanted, do no work and get stoned. They were not looking for promotion. Already neck deep in schemes, they were the underclass before that term was coined, living in the black market and doing very nicely thank you: fighting, drugging and partying their way through their teens, living like millionaires while they were still on the dole. Needless to say they were not at work for very long.

A band was the obvious extension of this lifestyle. They saw what good times other bunches of blaggers were having and decided that it was time to sign up, to join in. The group was built around a one-fingered keyboardist, Paul Davies; a great guitar-player who would slap the weirdest riffs into songs and give them a lop-sided Beefheart edge (that no one ever seemed to notice) called Mark Day; and a drummer called Gary Whelan, who had once had football trials for Man United before getting involved in this bacchanalian gang of outlaws.

Ryder took the vocals because he couldn't play anything and his brother Paul picked up the bass. It was a mad shambles – they just made it up as they went along and somehow it worked; whether they meant it or not they were completely original. The trump card was Mark Berry, a gangling youth, who was born in Liverpool and whose dad was a cop. He couldn't play or sing a note. Unlikely credentials for a key player in a band, but Berry or 'Bez' became a totem (pole) for a generation.

Bez may have, on paper, done fuck all, but could this cat dance. His weird, warped shapes – spaz-dancing like a refugee on space-age drugs – were aped by every wired teen in the late eighties. His bug-eyed expression and leering semi-grin just said one word. Drugs. In a pop scene riddled with wannabe outlaws, Bez was the real dad.

The Mondays faffed around for years and no one ever took any notice of them. They played crap local gigs, sat on the outside of a scene dominated by The Smiths and had no idea of how to get their band going in music-biz terms. They once went all the way to Blackpool to the seedy backstreet GPO club and entered a battle of bands. What the club regulars made of this slipshod, leftfield funk played by a bunch of the wildest, most wired football hoo-ligans in the country, makes the mind boggle. No, they didn't win.

The Happy Mondays were a million miles away from everyone. They didn't look like rock stars; they were dressed in their street duds, they had tightly cropped hair, they had none of the flamboyance of 'conventional' rock stars. They had their own code, their own sense of humour, they smoked endless joints and took piles of drugs. Their lifestyle was at total odds with the mid-eighties, when everyone was going on about 'Live Aid' and pop's mission to save the planet. They promised nobody nothing, they offered no solutions and gave no apologies.

Eventually they managed to get someone to manage them. Phil Saxe – who once sold them flares at his underground market stall in Manchester city centre – was a fast-talking hustler who seemed like one of them but a bit older; he seemed perfect for the job and was offered it. Saxe had no ideas about pop management but took the offer anyway. He got them into a Haçienda battle of the bands where, through a bit of skulduggery, they came to the attention of local TV presenter and head of Factory records, Tony Wilson.

Wilson was looking for his Sex Pistols. He'd had critical acclaim for Joy Division who had mutated into the perfect pop machine of New Order; his label Factory was credible, arty and oozed an image of slick, cold-hearted knowingness. What was required was something to mess up the formulae, a gang of street kids, urchins with a gobful of real life to spit into the sanitized eye of the eighties.

The key note here was eclecticism. Sure, they had roots in punk – most hooligans in their twenties in the mid-eighties had been fired by the rough-arsed tomfoolery of punk rock – but they had moved a long way since then.

If there was one band which defined that Manchester love of the off-the-wall, it was the Mondays. They had record tastes that spanned genres, they had no interest in boxing themselves in anywhere. In a city where it was not uncommon for someone to have a mariachi record, next to a metal record, next to a funk record, next to a blues album, while a freaked soul record boomed from the turntable, the Mondays would be the new kings.

There was the psychedelic funk gobbledy-gook of Parliament/Funkadelic and the urgent driving bass-lines of Northern Soul. They mashed this up with the Beatles and the Stones and then recycled tunes from wherever they could find them. Hip-hop (and later house) outfits were sampling slabs of the past and spitting them out as future, and now bands could do the same. Instead of using samplers they recycled melodies and lyrics and slotted them into their own songs where they pleased. It's already there, just grab what you want and stick it back together again, in your own way.

The thing was, they sounded utterly original; no other band on the scene sounded remotely like them. They were playing ramshackle, crazy, bad-ass funk that sounded like it came from the North and was played by some sneering top boys. So you got Clinton-esque warped jams with a stream-of-consciousness lyric spewed over the top.

Except this time it was from the north of England and it brought along its own mythology. Ryder, who to this day claims that he has no interest in his lyrics, could churn out hilarious spiels of surrealism, mangled by his half-cut northern drawl. Dirty jokes rubbed shoulders with pithy observation, and gave way to obscenity and gutter filth. They sounded like a kitchen-sink drama on acid, a drug-fuelled barrage of northernness delivered in that whiny non-voice, perfect for the loping, staggering music that thundered away in the background; songs driven by brother Paul's great bass-lines, always inventive and always melodic. They had funk and if you were as bombed as the band you could dance to it.

Their debut single, 'Delightful', came out in September 1985. It was produced by Mike Pickering and sounds as out of place now as it did then: a bumbling, snotty-sleeved bounce. The B-side was called 'Oasis': possibly mere coincidence, but a curator of British pop like Noel Gallagher would hardly have missed this. They followed this in August 1986 with the aptly named 'Freaky Dancing' and then a year later with 'Tart Tart' – great slices of stub-toed pop, that no one anywhere could get a handle on.

The debut album – the splendidly titled *Squirrel and G-Man Twenty Four Hour Party People Plastic Face Carnt Smile (White Out)* – was murdered by the ex-Velvet Underground Jon Cale's awful production. He had been appointed by Tony Wilson – a Velvet Underground fanatic – and totally dried out the sound. The songs themselves were great, more grinding funk-drenched slabs of oddness.

The record came out and disappeared. It wasn't like there was anyone out there that was going to buy into this sort of stuff; the Mondays were out to lunch. There simply wasn't a scene receptive enough. Way, way out of tune with the banal pop mainstream, they were not even that digestible by the underground scene (which at the time was far too po-faced and art-school to enjoy their shambolic, madcap gig antics).

What was needed was a cultural sea-change.

The next album was *Bummed* which, under the tutelage of Martin Hannett, was a far better sounding record. Hannett was a legendary Manchester producer: his style of total over-production, treating and twisting every sound with a barrage of effects, was not always that effective. With the Mondays, though, he hit bullseye.

October 1988's *Bummed* was a great rough-arsed northern pop record with titles like 'Some Cunt From Preston (Country

Song)', a filthy leering pun on 'Some country and western', it was taking no prisoners. It also contained 'Wrote For Luck'. Released just before the album, the single would spend the next year mutating into a pop monster. On release it seemed that it was going to disappear into a void. House music and E had scheduled their big coming-out/marriage reception for 1988. That summer the Haçienda became a temple of hedonism. Riotous nights of partying turned it into a sweat-stained home of energized dance celebration. This was a defining pop moment. The demand was for new groups who could relate to the new dance framework, groups who took the right drugs and wore the new, looser styles. And who was in the middle of this mêlée dealing out the new wonder drug? Yup, the town's arch-hustlers, the Happy Mondays, making a few quid selling the pills and necking a fair quantity themselves.

The new generation still wanted bands but they needed bands who talked the new talk and walked the new walk. In Manchester that meant the Stone Roses and particularly the Happy Mondays. *Bummed*'s sales rode the slipstream of a new dance-crazed rush.

The Happy Mondays remixed 'Wrote For Luck' releasing it as 'WFL' in September 1989, aiming their huge loping anthem at the dancefloor. It detonated with its thumping, rolling gait, its very pimp-roll of a beat was perfect for the times. Ryder's bruised vocal sounded like a five-in-the-morning yob yelling his head off, coming down and back home from a party. The fucked-up youth of Britain grinned and grooved to its gloriously inane refrain. This was a moment of pop perfection. It was the street anthem of the year.

And what a year 1989 was: a whirl of raves, crazed clubs and mental gigs; the Mondays on the road that year were a non-stop party of pills, thrills and bellyaches. Bez would dance for five minutes and then slump, bollocksed by the massive heat pouring off the crowd. Just watching the band ooze the groove and marvel at the ever-growing monster of 'Wrote For Luck' as it ended another climactic set was the most fun you could have at the back end of 1989.

This band defied all conventional theories of pop punditry; they had none of the so called advantages that pop bands should have. They were a bad-breathed slap of reality and street and they packed a bounce that made everyone in the room dance. At their peak in that year they, along with the Stone Roses, seemed untouchable, pop perfection.

Of course it would all get poisoned; it could never last; it was bound to fall in on itself. Not for another year though. The next album, *Pills 'n' Thrills and Bellyaches* was their most commercial, packed 'n' with great tunes. It may have lacked the roughshod charms of *Bummed* but it was their best received record, the one that the square kids could take home. It was the moment when house and rock were perfectly fused into pop. It spawned another brace of hits.

It was after this that the Mondays let other drugs dominate their workspace; stuff like smack and coke and crack started to creep into the band more and more. They had always messed with hard stuff, but the drugs were beginning to get in the way. They went to the Bahamas to record their final album, *Yes, Please!*, produced by the ex-Talking Heads rhythm section of Tina Weymouth and Chris Frantz. They battled on as Bez kept crashing cars, getting his arm into a bizarre metallic sling and Shaun Ryder sat on the bog smoking the crack pipe.

The theory was that the Bahamas would keep the band away from drugs. But these guys were experts, full-on party animals. They found even more drugs than usual. The band may have kept their noses relatively clean (so to speak) but the Ryder brothers and Bez were getting severely fucked up. The recording of the record was a shambles.

It was too slickly produced to be a proper Mondays album; the beats were Americanized and they had lost the lolloping gait that had trademarked them. Despite the crazy recording schedules they delivered an almost AOR record. Even that didn't stop the sleaze from dribbling through their last single, 'Stinkin Thinking', a trawl through the comedown of smack.

And that was it. There was one last tour where the support band Stereo MCs stole the show and the Mondays collapsed in on themselves. EMI attempted to sign them and Shaun Ryder walked out to 'get a Kentucky's', which was slang for something spicier. EMI threatened to pull out and in one last, cold and miserable meeting Ryder sat down with the rest of the band in manager McGough's Manchester Office. He implored the band to stick together to pull off one last scam and take the money from EMI. Paul Ryder looked at him and said, 'You know, Shaun, no one wants to work with you any more, it's over.' And the band crumbled.

There was little more that they could do. They were on the slide in the UK and the States just wasn't getting it. Trying to sell this band to the Americans was a nightmare. Football hooligans? Ecstasy? Crossing stuff over? Twisting my melons?! What can you mean, maaan? This was a very British disease.

The Mondays were a success of their time. They appeared when pop gave an inch and allowed some real madness to sneak into the charts. It happens now and then. When will the dullards next move over and give the crazies – or maybe we should say the inspired – a crack of the whip?

Part Three

14

I Know It's Over

Chris managed to put everything to do with the Rain and the lads out of his mind for a couple of months. He had the videos of United's European triumphs to fill the nights which once had been occupied with rehearsals; then there was his new place, which needed redecorating and restoring. He didn't see the lads in the pubs at all. Once or twice it occurred to him that they were probably getting it together in some basement somewhere but the experiences of May had left him too drained to care. So when a mate phoned in early August to see if he wanted to see 'Liam's band' debut at the Boardwalk, he declined. Whatever curiosity he felt took second place to the desire to get those last rolls of Anaglypta up.

He shrugged when he heard they'd changed their name from the Rain to Oasis. 'What the fuck is "Oasis" supposed to signify?' he wondered. Later, he learned that his mates Tony French and Chris Johnson had been there when the band and its hangers-on sat

185 ■

around suggesting names. Chris J had popped up with 'Oasis' at random. Nothing to do with a poster for a Swindon leisure centre at all. A swift bit of copyrighting, and Chris J's fortune would've been assured.

One Burnage boy who didn't turn down the invite was Noel Gallagher. However lame the band were that night – and they were clearly under-rehearsed, as well as underwhelmed by playing to only 46 people after they'd done 300 with the Rain – Noel had seen something. Not, perhaps, his brother's star quality: there was little in evidence that night as Liam sang flat and without confidence, while gooning about like a lobotomized Brown. But it was a ready-made band, clearly without proper direction and therefore begging for leadership. As such, it was a rarity: bands whose rhythm sections have become tight and hard-wearing like this one had are normally never on offer for takeover. Virtually by definition, their quality comes from a sustained period of leadership and mission, which in the Rain's case had come at least partly from Chris. To catch the rest of the band at that moment, fresh from decapitation, is difficult. Most bands, having progressed so far, do not then undergo the sort of transformation the Rain/early Oasis were about to have wrought upon them.

What few appreciate is how vital it was for Noel at that moment to be able to find a vehicle like this. For the curse of the musical loner, who has some sense of vision and a back-pack full of songs like Noel brought home, is that it is so hard to get a band together. Especially when part of the vision you have seen involves the creation of a 'real' band, that is to be musically driven, tight together and apparently unmanufactured. Noel's vision, viewed objectively, was a pop project implanted into a rock milieu, using the language and imagery of classic rock lineage but actually pressing all the pop buttons in the national audience. Result: you clean up in both domains. Radio-friendly melodicism captures the casual punter, who couldn't care less whether their tunes come from 'shallow' pop acts or 'proper' rock bands. And the so-called serious music fan can enjoy the music despite the pop appeal because it's coming from a 'real band', who appear to be as genuine an article as, say, the Manics or Joy Division.

Noel arguably came to that Oasis gig like a svengali checking out a local disco-dolly outfit, looking for a vehicle that could be repainted in his colours, ready to drive his songs to Number One. He takes them over, wrests complete compositional control, dictates the arrangements and repertoire, changes their musical style, tells them how to behave on stage, insists they replicate recorded sound note-for-note on stage . . . The reason some people accuse Oasis of having no soul is partly founded on this truth: that, after January 1992, they ceased to develop like a classic rock band is supposed to and became a pop-writer's project dressed in the garb of rock classicism. The answer to that is:

who cares, it works. Ironically, without the period they spent with Chris Hutton, a period they now seek to ignore, this sleight-of-hand could not have succeeded. Because most of Oasis came up the 'proper way' – that is, being a product of shared influences, coming from the same area, all contributing to the artistry and vision and so on – our attention is successfully diverted from their post-1992 surrender to an outsider's imposed vision and Masterplan.

What else could Noel do but take on the group? He was 24 and had never been in a band; it was too late to go in at the ground floor and build one up from its roots in the ideologically correct fashion. Putting one together from unknown elements was clearly fraught with danger – as the story of the Rain demonstrates, musical units are hard enough to sustain even when the members are mates. A load of sessioneers was out of the question, completely contrary to his 'classic rock' vision and an open invitation to critical mauling once the *NME* smelled fakery. Even if he were able to find possible band members out in the community, what self-respecting artist would go into a new venture which demanded immediate surrender of personal creative ambitions and total subservience to one overwhelmingly dominant member?

Here was a ready-made unit, built up in classic fashion, currently under the sway of Liam's dominant personality which in turn could easily be manipulated by his older brother. He knew all the members, they came from his manor and, it soon transpired, could be won over by virtue of the fact that his own songs were more commercial than theirs. And in 'Live Forever', he had one song that was also clearly artistically superior to their efforts too. He was offering a sense of mission, a book full of music-biz contacts and expertise learned at the feet of the master businessmen in the Inspirals and a bit of lead guitar as well. All they had to do was go along with Noel's artistic vision – which did not include their contribution – in exchange for the promise of a much greater chance in the marketplace. All four were ready to deal, and no one mentioned Faust.

By Christmas, with the Burnage pubs' party season in full staggering swing, Chris was back on top, buzzing off United's charge to the top of the league and making plans for a mad parachute jump session with Tony French and the Moran brothers. He knew Tony was doing a bit of design work for Oasis but it was no problem; and he had to admit that the swirl logo Tony had come up with was sound. So when he bumped into Guigs during a wild night at the Milestone, he felt able to offer a couple of cool pleasantries. Guigs was guarded and reserved but dropped the latest bit of news: Noel Gallagher was joining the band full-time. In the meantime, they were rehearsing for a demo of the songs Bonehead and Liam had written together. A few months later, Guigs turned up at the parachute session and played the lads the tape on his car stereo. Strangely, he seemed keen to gauge Chris's reaction, but now it was Chris's turn to be noncommittal. Privately, he thought Liam sounded poor: clearly lacking confidence and his own distinct 'voice', too concerned to ape Ian Brown's stylisms. But to say so would have sounded bitter and churlish.

Nevertheless, Chris's curiosity was growing. What would they be like live? Watching Oasis would allow him to do something he could never have done as a singer – be in the audience to see what 'his own' band were like. And he liked Bonehead's music as much as ever: 'Alice', 'Reminisce' and especially 'Take Me' all hit the mark, even if the lyrics were dreadful. But wasn't that lead guitar a bit clichéd and dull? Perhaps he'd been spoiled by Marr and Squire – this was how mortals played. Anyway, remarked Guigs, 'Noel will be writing our songs from now on.' And Noel's virtuosity would be in writing notes, not bending them.

15

Unloveable

Has history been crueller to any band in recent memory than it has to the poor Inspiral Carpets? You can go round Manchester for hours and not find a single soul who'll admit ever having liked them. Yet you can bet half of them will have spent some part of 1989 in a Moo! T-shirt and will have undoubtedly frugged frenziedly to 'Find Out Why' every club night for most of August.

Manchester now likes to remind you that the Inspirals were actually from Oldham. Say no more: virtually sheep-shaggers, eh? No wonder they had a fixation with a barnyard animal. And it's undoubtedly true that the emergence of the Roses and Mondays onto a national stage suddenly made the Inspirals look like the runts of the pack, Madchester's embarrassing Dave Clark Five. By the time of Spike Island, an Inspirals beanie was about as old hat as you could get.

They cried all the way to the bank, of course. Whilst

the Roses wasted their zenith years and the Mondays blew themselves off the summit, the Inspirals survived, milking every last dollar out of the States and Japan once Britain had rejected them. The changing perception of their infamous 'business heads' typified the public's attitudes. Where once they'd been held up as a shining example of Mancunian can-do spirit and free-trade initiative, now they became capitalist running dogs, more concerned with big bucks than art. Singer Tom, whose dominant voice was once described as 'a clarion call across the tower-block rooftops', was later pilloried as the most grating foghorn since Tony Hadley. And so it went on. The brutality of a critical backlash is that precisely all those distinguishing facets which once apparently made you great are then inverted to become gross indulgences. The Inspirals never made a great album but they produced a ground-breaking EP in '88 and two classic singles in '89, for which they deserve some credit.

Noel Gallagher's attitude to them was, therefore, fairly typical. In '88, he'd been enough of a fan to audition as their singer and then grateful enough for the chance to tour with them as a roadie. Hilarious pictures of Noel in a bowl haircut, holding hands with Clint Boon, are testament enough. But by 1991, he was openly derisive of them, hooting behind their backs, gathering experience and contacts until he could get his own act together. (Traces, perhaps, of the way in which Noel denigrated Tony McCarroll while keeping him in the band for the best part of two years.) His time with the Carpets proved to be invaluable; you could even argue that they were the most influential of all the Manchester bands for Noel.

First, he emerged as a committed Beatles fan, with obvious consequences for his songwriting. Second, he'd learned the ropes about the logistics and politics of operating a rock band, allowing him to short-circuit the usual painful on-job training and hit the ground running with Oasis. Thirdly, the conservative and business-like Inspirals philosophy had removed any last vestiges of Punk-like revolutionary spirit. Noel came back committed to order, discipline and planning, to an almost frighteningly intense degree.

So, Oasis would not follow the Pistols route, i.e. seat-of-the-pants flying which could crash at any moment. His band would stick to the masterplan, precluding momentary inspiration and experimental detours. They would have a proper, efficient power-structure, with himself at the apex, and a long-term release schedule to maximize resources. Fucking about and self-destructive behaviour (though not, apparently, including coke abuse) were forbidden. Oasis would be a band that always turned up on time, gave professional performances and stuck to recording session time-frames.

Much of this is a core reason for Oasis's success. There is a secure reliability and hard-headed business sense about them that plays well with the music-biz. The danger of subservience to this level-headed, button-down philosophy – leaving aside the obvious probability that it will produce safe, con-servative records – is that you could end up placing business above art. The recording of the *Morning Glory* album, as most participants have admitted, was wildly rushed, leaving songs under-developed and perfunctorily performed to the detriment of its over-all quality. A bolshier, less business-like band would have told the world to shove it, burned the tapes and retired to the country for a rethink before re-embarking on new sessions. But Oasis had a schedule to follow, a deadline to meet, fans' expectations to fulfil: they did what they could and released it, despite knowing it could have been better. Com-mercially, it didn't matter, but that is not the point. As Noel himself now seems to recognize by taking nearly two years before releasing the new album, art and commerce have nothing at all to do with each other.

However much Noel and others might seek to down-play the Carpets' influence, every Oasis fan should pay their respects to the Inspirals for their role in Noel's development. There was only one thing they couldn't help him with: how to cope when you've got a Liam Gallagher in your band. For much of the above is anathema to a punk spirit like his and it's no surprise that all the threatened derailments of the Oasis bandwagon have derived from Liam's inability to follow the Noel rule-book. Many might suggest that this is Liam's most attractive asset, eyebrows included; Noel must see it as their Achilles heel. A spirit he may admire from afar, as once he admired the Pistols from the safety of 1983; but Achillean all the same.

16

I Started Something
I Couldn't Finish

Chris didn't see Oasis at the Boardwalk in January '92;
he'd assumed he'd hardly have been welcome anyway.
Later, he was told that Liam and Guigsy had claimed
to have been round to his house in December, bearing
gig tickets as some sort of peace offering, only to find
Chris wasn't in. 'So why didn't they leave the tickets
for me?' wondered Chris. Smacked of propaganda to
him: good ol' Oasis, looking after a past comrade. More
typical was Liam's cheek back in September when he
mooched around to Chris's to try and blag his mike and
stand, the subtext of his request being 'Well, you're
not gonna need 'em now anyway, are ya?' (Liam
always did have plenty of front.) As it happened,
most of Chris's gear had been nicked or 'permanently
borrowed', so he genuinely couldn't help. Not that
he'd have wanted to, of course. Equally typical was
Guigsy's failure to invite Chris to his 21st birthday
piss-up in May, an event which most of Burnage

would expect to turn up to. Chris tagged along and got in anyhow.

(His curiosity to see how the band were doing outweighed his fear of the piss-taking he was going to receive after United's catastrophic failure to win the 1992 League title, handed to Leeds amidst trauma and Fergie fuckwittery. He still hadn't forgotten the infamy of the night in 1989 when City beat United 5-1, when he was the only Red in Burnage to show his face in the pubs. Blues from miles around, whom he'd not seen in ages, came out especially to see the sight; Guigsy made a 5–1 neck-chain of shame which he ceremonially hung around Chris's neck in front of the entire, whooping Milestone crowd. Blues queued up to try out their 'hilarious' jokes on him, many settling for 'What's the time? Five past Leighton!' and its derivatives. He got off lightly this time – even Bitter Blues can be sufficiently human to know when a bloke's had enough.)

Chris and Guigs avoided each other but Bonehead's characteristic blithe charm made him approachable enough – he even invited Chris to come down and watch their regular rehearsals at the Boardwalk. A mention of the Happy Mondays, who were rumoured to be in serious difficulties out in the Caribbean, triggered a news release from Bonehead: 'Factory tried to sign us, y'know. We turned 'em down – they were takin' the piss, offering a completely shite deal.' Chris expressed amazement that, however poor the offer, Oasis should have turned down such an apparently blue-chip company.

Bonehead grinned malevolently, perhaps remember-
ing the Rain's experience chez Wilson: 'Listen, the
Mondays are blowing a million quid, Northside are
picking up two hundred quid a week for doing fuck
all and New Order might have split for all we know.
Face it: Factory are going nowhere. They've got fuck
all. If Northside's your best hope, the future ain't so
bright is it?'

It wouldn't be too long before Bonehead was proved
completely right. The state of the Mondays, as reflected
in the useless *Yes, Please!* album finally released in
October, was symptomatic of the way Manchester had
lost the initiative, and the plot. Factory Records and
the Haçienda/New Order empire surrounding it had
never been less influential. The Roses, already three
years from their debut's release, were only at the stage
of signing their new Geffen deal by March. The Mondays, whose previous album had seemed to establish
the indie-dance gold standard, had apparently been
comprehensively devalued by Primal Scream.

Indeed, despite the geographical dislocation, *Screamadelica* was touted as being the ultimate Madchester
manifesto, a classic benchmark against which *Yes Please!*
wilted impotently. (Actually, *Screamadelica* never really
tackled the immiscibility of indie-rock and dance,
instead largely dividing the record between the two.
Pills 'n' Thrills and Bellyaches was surely the more
genuine attempt at producing a new hybrid form
and has probably aged better.) Nevertheless, what did
Manchester have to offer in 1992: What Was The World

Waiting For, supposedly? Puressence, Molly Halfhead, That Uncertain Feeling and the Sugar Merchants – the least inspiring second wave of an invasion since Herman's Hermits and Dave Clark chased the Beatles across the Atlantic.

Counter-factual history is trendy these days, so imagine this: had the Roses managed to be conventional enough to release a second album around Xmas '91, one that followed from but also progressed beyond 'Fools Gold', such a definitive indie-pop-dance statement would have cleaned up worldwide. The painful pining we all endured as we waited for the Roses was for good reason – who doubted that this band could deliver the ultimate pop album? But they didn't; instead, Nirvana unleashed 'Teen Spirit' on the UK and the American domination of the musical moment was assured. 1992 became the year of grunge and 'rawk', draped in stars 'n' stripes, and proclaiming the Death of Pop.

Britain's only hopes, Blur, took one look around them, dumped the brilliant 'Popscene' on a bemused and ungrateful public, and exited stage left. They would need this year to find themselves, for their lack of definition and purpose had marred much of what they had released until now. Caught uncomfortably between the end of baggy, the middle of shoegazing and the beginning of Britpop, Leisure-era Blur meant nothing to anyone. Writers remarked that they were spokesmen for the Blank Generation who had nothing to say, save asking the price of effects pedals. With what could a Blur-ite respond? Blur were evidently drenched in talent and suss but had no function. Kurt Cobain and Brett Anderson combined to give Blur antagonistic, reactive purpose; they in turn, so ironically, provided the runway for Oasis's take-off. And, if you want to follow the circle all the way around, the Gallaghers' usurption of Blur's position as Number One UK Pop Gods has resulted in Blur travelling back to December '91 with 'Song 2'.

Even the Gallaghers appeared to be missing Blur in '92. Liam had apparently bought and enthused over a couple of their singles in '91 and Noel was in appreciative attendance at a Manchester Blur gig in '92. They hadn't sold the hall out, they seemed to have no direction, the world was ignoring them – but they were brilliant, on fire, as exciting as any of the Manchester greats. If it had occurred to the Gallaghers that Blur's problems spelled trouble for them too, they didn't show it, swaggering around the Middleton Hippodrome stage before Revenge in April with their customary arrogance. Their attitude always looked the part, which is half the battle when you're trying to get a deal, whether as an indie band or bunch of pop chart merchants. But at least during the spring of '92, the direction Oasis were promising to take seemed to threaten Blur-ish oblivion.

The increasing introduction of Noel's songs made them poppier, just at a time when pop seemed to be taboo. An irony struck Chris at the time: Nirvana's success would have made life so much easier for the Rain, had they persevered. In opting for Noel, Oasis seemed to have taken a step away from the zeitgeist. Because the Rain were doomier, rockier, harsher and more 'meaningful', they would have been precisely the kind of outfit a UK record company would've been looking for in early '92 to satisfy the demand Nirvana and others had exposed. Oasis, however, would have to weather the storm for at least another year – and would have to thank 'southern ponces' for their eventual opportunity.

There's a certain pleasing symbolic synchronicity in the cover of the *Melody Maker* during the week Oasis supported Revenge featuring 'The Best Band In Britain': Suede. It would be their success that allowed Oasis to become established, at least indirectly. But for a good six months yet, Suede could be dismissed by those convinced that the US hegemony was here for the duration. One good debut single in the lower reaches of the chart counted for nothing against millions of US-earned album sales. For those six months, Oasis were set against the grain, with only Factory showing even the slightest interest. Indeed, what was keeping them in the game appeared to be – Chris smiles wryly – the continuing influence of the Rain upon their sound and arrangements.

In mid-92, critics and audiences were entirely receptive to the rockier, doomier elements which hung over Oasis from their old days. Noel found his band facing comparisons to Nirvana/doom-rock which he didn't like but which were meant to be complimentary. The band's sound and repertoire were essentially a cross between classic early/mid-period Oasis and the Rain. Some of Noel's early, more primitive songs were indistinguishable in type from Bonehead's (whose 'Take Me' remained the most popular song in their set, even with Paul 'Bod' Gallagher). And as Noel's education of the band was not yet complete, large traces of the Rain's big-beast rawness remained – with the approval of the punters.

Liam later remarked, of an early September 1992 gig which typified this synthesis: 'I wish we could have recorded an album then: that's when we were really rocking.' Instead, all remaining drops of The Rain were removed. Oasis live eventually became the tight, buttoned-down writer's vehicle it is today rather than risk the semi-uncontrolled self-expression of the 'live experience' type of band.

Oasis were going to be headlining at the Boardwalk for the first time on July 14, 1992. Chris preferred to watch them rehearse a few weeks earlier than go to the gig, just as Bonehead had invited him to do. He hadn't seen Tony Mac since the split and the drummer looked faintly embarrassed to see Chris mosey up to the front of the rehearsal room. Chris thought it telling, characteristically anyway – Tony had had little to do with his ousting, yet he looked the most shame-faced of the four. Increasingly, Chris would feel that Tony was actually the best bloke out of all of them, and wished he'd got to know him better earlier.

The rehearsal started, under Noel's strict direction. It would be the first time Chris had ever seen Liam sing, his usurper in action. It occurred to him that they'd simply swapped positions; he was stood precisely where Liam used to watch the Rain's rehearsals at Raffles over a year before. But this was a very different band he was watching. Sure, he could hear much of what they once shared in garages and clubs in Burnage; Guigs had improved a little but the Rain rhythm was as primal as ever. Yet Noel was so utterly in control – was this the kind of band they'd all wanted? He couldn't get over how quiet Guigsy was, apparently in total deference to Noel; speechless even. Bonehead would pipe up from time to time with suggestions and it looked as though he might still retain some element of power within the band. Otherwise, this was the 100 per cent Noel Gallagher Experience.

For an hour, virtually all he could hear was Noel's voice barking orders, shouting chord patterns, chiding others' mistakes. Chris double-checked the bass drum skin, just to see if it now said 'Noel and the Oasis' or somesuch. A wry reflection: all that private railing against Liam for 'stealing his band' had been a tad inaccurate. The only take-over tycoon here was Noel. He even muttered to himself: 'Jesus, this is Noel and four puppets.' For the only time since April '91, he felt a twinge of sympathy for Bonehead and Guigs. This wasn't the democratic, collaborative joint venture they'd planned as Burnage lads back in 1990. Had they given up on everything they'd wanted to do artistically?

Then, as what he later discovered to be 'D'Yer Wanna Be A Spaceman' kicked in, he realized something else that answered his question. Noel was going to make this happen; he knew exactly what he was doing. Chris realized Noel had the contacts, that he'd seen how a successful band was run. He'd learned well at the feet of the Inspirals, the ex-employers whom Noel was slagging off repeatedly throughout the rehearsal. And he had some songs there which would sell. They weren't Chris's personal cup of tea, and he would have been surprised if they'd been Guigs' and Bonehead's either; but he knew enough about music to appreciate the all-conquering power of a catchy chorus. As Liam jigged about, singing better than he had on the demo-tape though physically still in thrall to Ian Brown's stage style, Chris felt the first pangs of something he'd hoped to avoid – jealousy.

It passed, once he'd convinced himself that he couldn't have been happy artistically in such a dictatorial set-up; yet for a few moments he'd glimpsed the future. Noel would make it, using the band he'd built, and they'd all be rich and successful without him. The saint has not yet been canonized who wouldn't have succumbed to the green-eyed monster upon such a realization. Only Bonehead engaged Chris in conversation afterwards (Guigsy scuttled off smartly): 'So, what do you think of us?' grinned Bonehead toothily. 'Yeah, all right,' smiled Chris, through gritted grinding teeth. And 'all right' was about as high as Chris's opinion of Oasis's music ever got, for within another year, they'd bear scarcely any resemblance musically or spiritually to the band he once led.

One mystery remained for Chris: why had they replaced him with Liam? Technically, he didn't yet seem to be a better singer; they both sounded equally Mancunian; were equally popular with the girls; and behind the mike, Liam was still too unoriginal, relying heavily on Brownisms. Chris even wondered whether this was what Liam had been doing at all those Rain rehearsals and gigs – watching someone else learn the ropes so that he might short-circuit the learning process later. That would have been a bitter irony: to have helped with part of Liam's frontman tuition, only to see the pupil turn the tables upon graduation. But Chris could see that if Liam didn't get himself sorted with a style of his own, Oasis would not prosper. The intensity of the media/fan focus on any group's singer doesn't permit gauche imperfection. Liam could see it too. By November, he'd have found his voice and stance by being utterly natural: untutored and unyielding in both, to original effect.

Eventually, Chris would be told by those around Oasis that Liam's coup had had more to do with Noel than any innate promise Liam possessed. The approved story of Oasis posits that Noel's introduction was almost by chance, that had he been in the States in August 1991, Oasis would have continued without him, conceivably for good. But the story Chris is now given makes more sense. This suggests it was always in Liam's mind to entice his brother into his band, as far back as the winter of 90/91 when Liam originally targeted the Rain for take-over.

Moreover, the whisperers say Liam pitched Noel's name into the equation early on at Raffles rehearsals – that was the reason for the mysterious huddles Chris would sometimes find when he came into the room. If Guigs and Bonehead were turning Liam's offers down at first, then at least the seeds of doubt had been planted. They all knew Noel was, comparatively speaking, a big-shot; any band would want to have him in the loop, without even beginning to take account of his songwriting. Chris didn't know it but at the first sign of treading water – such as April '91, supposedly – the Rain's other two founder members would have another route open to them. And it was certainly widely rumoured in Burnage throughout the autumn that Noel was inevitably going to join Oasis, long before the brothers' deal was formally agreed.

Such a scenario would at least explain why Guigs and Bonehead agreed to overthrow an established and popular singer in favour of an unknown whom they'd never heard in action and who had no track-record. If this reveals a rational calculation behind the behaviour of Guigs and Bonehead – whether this brings them credit or shame is up to the reader – then it certainly shows a clever and canny side to Liam which has not otherwise been overly apparent to Oasis-watchers . . .

On November 22, Liam further demonstrated this unacknowledged smartness when he led Oasis onto the Boardwalk stage once more. Gone was the gawky, clumsy monkeying about and blatantly Brownish vocal stylisms; instead, he chose to remain largely motionless, keening up towards the mike to allow more of his natural voice out. What he lost, in appearing to be blanker and less interactive, he easily regained by projecting an image of arrogant self-confidence and a plangent vocal tone more akin to the Liam we recognize today. Simply, he seemed cooler and more self-assured, possessing his own persona rather than an amalgamation co-opted from predecessors. With Noel's newer songs now dominant in the set, Oasis were banging on 1993's door, the past year's uneasiness contradictions behind them.

It had been a week for swaggering arrivals all round. Four days after the gig, Eric Cantona entered his new kingdom at Old Trafford, another heavy-browed brooding frontman for Manchester to get used to. The physical and attitudinal resemblances between Liam and Eric have been often noted, though no-one will ever expect Liam (or indeed most football fans) to share the French god's interests in nineteenth century poetry. For once, Liam's Bitter-Blueness subsided enough for him to admit two things: one, that Eric seemed to be a bit of a star; and two, that 'You Munich bastards are going to win the League with him.' Right both times, Bertie Magoo.

For the next six months or so, just about the only

issue Chris and Liam would agree on was 'That Eric Cantona's a geezer.' In May, United and Eric finally broke the Reds' 26-year failure to win the League when Aston Villa lost to Oldham. Liam was on hand to yell at Chris across a football field: 'What's it like to be gifted the League, you lucky cunts?' Liam fumed and muttered about United all evening, taking it very badly for such a self-confessed part-timer. Liam was the kind of light Blue who couldn't even name City's scorers in their 'glorious' 1976 League Cup victory. Ancient history, of course, the last time City won a trophy – still, something a truer Blue like Noel has engraved on his heart.

Funnily enough, when Chris and Steve Shenton saw Noel on Albert Square next day, he was remarkably generous. Despite the fact that the Red next to Chris, perched up on top of the statue, had just chucked a can at him, Noel yelled, 'Congratulations, you Red bastards; about fuckin' time I suppose.' He was a very brave Bluenose to be out and about at all, as 40,000 pissed-up Reds gathered for the celebration match against Blackburn. But by the end of the month, Noel would have secured his own title of sorts. After Oasis's first successful away games in Liverpool and Glasgow, they'd finally come to the attention of an enthusiastic Alan McGhee, supremo at influential independent label Creation. It was the equivalent of a non-leaguer getting plucked off the playing fields by Alex Ferguson.

17

Money Changes Everything

From around September 1992 until the summer of 1993, Chris was always quick to discover news first-hand of the latest Oasis developments for a simple yet remarkable reason. Despite everything that had happened, despite the fact that Chris no longer saw Oasis socially, the lads and their entourages would still congregate like the faithful for football matches virtually every week. How could Oasis or Chris play with each other, like kids without a care in the world, given the seething resentments under the surface? But as Chris explained, this was football. The game always mattered to them more than anything else – even part-timer Liam became a 100-per-cent-er when it came to playing. For working-class lads (and now, increasingly, middle-class blokes too), football is the great unifier.

Look at any group of lads going to the match together year after year. They may have become divided over politics, music, religion; some may have married, turned to crime or slipped into the dole underclass; some may have moved to completely different areas, or out of the city altogether. But the game will continue to reunite them, as they meet up for Saturday sessions in the Dog & Partridge or Claremont. And as long as the talk stays football-centred, they'll get on as as well as ever. In playing the game, rivalries can temporarily be forgotten, as all that matters is how your passes link up. Besides, Chris had been determined to take everything that had happened stoically, like a man. He was never one to bear grudges.

Late 1992 meant Tuesday-night football down at the Pitz in Ardwick, which had 12 pitches for community use. Oasis F.C. rarely missed a session. Chris, Guigs, Liam and Chris Johnstone were ever-presents – unfortunately, so was the rotund Bod Gallagher, Chris's least favourite Gallagher. Being on the porky side meant Bod had to go in goal, always the worst punishment in playground football. (Strangely, for such a big City fan, Bod always wore a Celtic top, despite that team traditionally being the favoured Glasgow choice of United fans.) Still, he hadn't yet picked up any of the attitude for which he is now well-known. The next time Chris ran into Bod, at a Black Grape gig years later, he couldn't believe the transformation. Bod appeared to Chris to have become the big 'I Am', name-dropping, expecting star treatment and ordering Chris and co. 'not to call me Bod – my name's Paul'. Later he would tell one of them, 'Oasis are my brothers – and that's it. The rest are nothing.'

In March '93, the boys started to meet up for Sunday matches on the fields closer to home. Tony Mac became a regular and even Noel took time off writing to come down for a game. Chris, graciously, took the opportunity to tell Noel he'd enjoyed their January Boardwalk gig and the party afterwards. He'd have told Guigsy, except he felt that his old mate was avoiding eye contact and keeping silent. Chris took a certain pleasure in seeing Guigs' continued discomfiture, and he admits that when they ended up on opposing sides, his own tackles on Guigs might just have carried that extra bite . . .

Watching Oasis F.C. in action, one couldn't help noticing how well their playing roles fitted their personalities. Guigs fancied himself as a solid midfielder; quite an intelligent passer, quietly effective and with decent vision of the overall picture. Bizarrely, his Maine Road hero as a teenager had been Ian Bishop, always the target of the most scurrilous chants at Old Trafford for reasons we'd better not explore. On the field, Guigsy liked to pretend he was Mike Doyle, the seventies mainstay reputed to be the hardest Blue on the staff (ask Lou Macari). Noel, when he turned up, took the commander's role, plonking himself just forward of the centre-circle, letting the workhorses do the running while he picked out the cunning balls.

Liam, simply, was the biggest goal-hanging glory-hunting striker in Burnage, with a non-stop commentary mouth like Alan Shearer. 'He certainly knew where the goal was,' remarked Chris, 'mainly because he was always stood in it.' On special days, Liam would wear his 1969 FA Cup Final jersey, the striped classic in which Neil Young beat Peter Shilton. Playing Summerbee to his Young out on the wing was Tony Mac (who's nonetheless a Red), bounding down the touchline before thumping balls across for Liam to avoid heading. As most games tended to descend into midfield skirmishing, Tony would spend more time than most out in the cold, as usual. And then there was Chris, a bone-crunching no-nonsense centre-half: reliable, hard and always in the thick of it. Chris's hero was always Bryan Robson, though Liam likened his playing style to that of notorious England warrior Terry Butcher. Like Butcher, Chris was never happier than when leaving the field with blood all over his shirt. Guigs knew the score and never came near him. Liam soon learned.

They'd had a particularly rough game one Sunday. Chris and Liam were on opposing teams and the scores were level. For once, Liam was outside the six-yard box, with his marker Chris lurking yards away. Guigs knocked a through-ball past the line – suddenly, it was Liam versus Chris, with every other player a blood-thirsty spectator. Chris never bottled a 50/50 tackle, everyone knew that. The two were on collision course. Whether everything that had happened in the Rain was welling up within, Chris couldn't say, but he felt himself go in harder than ever before. Liam tried to bottle out, having seen the murderous intent, but couldn't fully escape. Chris didn't just take him out: Liam was sent flying and spinning cartoonishly, to be deposited in a crumpled heap some distance away. 'I won the ball!' grinned Chris at his slack-jawed colleagues. Even today, Chris can't play on those fields without someone coming up to him to mention 'that Liam tackle'. As an impressed team-mate marvelled, 'That was Norman Whiteside class', which Chris ranks as the highest compliment possible.

Fortunately for Oasis, Liam was bruised but unbroken and recovered to play the Wah Wah Hut in Glasgow two weeks later. Burnage's playing fields wouldn't be seeing much more of Oasis from now on; after June '93, Oasis were constantly on tour. When they did come back, however, Liam made sure he was on the same team as Chris . . .

It was on that football field that Chris learned Oasis had pulled off the big one. A shout from the touchline, early June: it was Tony Mac, running onto the pitch. 'Chris, guess what: we're gonna be signed! Creation are gonna sign us!' As Tony beamed in front of him, Chris had to feel pleased for him. Not for some of those other bastards, perhaps, but he congratulated Tony with genuine warmth. Tony shook his head in wonder: 'I can't believe it. They're actually going to pay us to do music. Unbelievable!'

Chris could believe it. He'd got a copy of the new Oasis demo, recorded at the Real People's studio, which included 'Whatever', 'Rock 'n' Roll Star' and

'Columbia'. No matter that he thought the first outrageously twee and the second clichéd: this was commercial stuff. He'd seen the January gig and recognized that Liam had successfully transferred his Burnage 'front' to the stage – which outsiders would soon call 'star quality', not knowing that such swaggering attitude is common currency in Manchester. And the band still had the drive they'd built during the Rain, the 4/4 rock power in the rhythm section that slashed all over the floppy fringes of old indie-pop. Although it would be another four months before they actually signed to Creation, and almost a year until their first big hit, he already knew they'd make it.

For apart from their intrinsic qualities, the band were now working with the grain. Blur's new album had found unanimous critical favour, clearly signalling that media support would exist for any new British band with pop-structured songs that could retake the charts. And the popular success of Suede had removed any doubts about British guitar-pop's commercial appeal. The bedlam across Britain which greeted Suede's tour in November had testified to that; their album's ascent to number one in April, breaking sales records in two weeks flat, had proved the point. 'Metal Mickey', for example, was virtually indistinguishable in atmosphere and musical typology from many Noel songs. If Suede could sell, so could Oasis. The 'curse' of Nirvana was being lifted.

Oasis would not be quite fast enough to take advantage

of the gap Suede left in late '93, as their album slowed down and critics searched for the Next Big Thing to continue the Brit revival. Indeed, they took a rare knock-back in December when the jewel in the *NME*'s critical crown, Johnny Cigarettes, panned their performance supporting St Etienne in Birmingham. Not only had he dismissed their gig but he'd sneered at their very essence, with a prominence in the taste-setting Review section that could not be missed. The boost they'd received back in July when the same journal's Emma Morgan had raved over them had been more than just cancelled out. Morgan was a teenage scribbler, a stringer, of no real influence. Cigarettes was a name, a presence (and built like a stormtrooper, as Bod sheepishly noted when the Gallaghers went looking for him before bottling out).

But despite Johnny's stand, the impetus appeared to be irrestistible. The *NME* printed a 'correcting' review of another Oasis gig that month, and the train was back on track. So confident were Noel and Guigs in the future that they'd both left Manchester during the autumn of '93 to set up homes in London. 'Fuck all that "roots" shit,' remarked one of them. The capital was where rock stars lived, right?

The rivals they would come to hate then did Oasis the biggest favour of their career. Blur dazzled Britain with two brilliant releases, 'Girls & Boys' and the *Parklife* album – 1994 was Blur's year, contest over, before it had a chance to reach spring. The LP which truly announced Britpop to the nation was never bettered

217 ■

within that canon, uniting critical and public opinion in fevered admiration like no other British album of the nineties. Its opening quartet in particular provided a barrage of pop exhilaration not felt since *Lexicon of Love*. If Blur hadn't exactly stolen Oasis's thunder – for the Gallaghers' project was not ready for proper launch yet anyway – they had established themselves as the incumbents who'd have to be dethroned. Yet they had also opened the pathway to Oasis in an even more marked way than Suede's success had done.

The public clearly wanted short, hummable bursts of energetic pop, laced with arrogance, delivered with laddish humour and suss, yet containing enough familiar echoes of past heroes to be comfortable rather than challenging. Above all, they subconsciously wanted Beatlisms. Blur's debts to the Fab Four were subtly different to Oasis's, of course. Blur took McCartneyesque observational techniques and a perfect pitch for stylish arrangements; Oasis took the chorus-releases and beat-group chordery. And while Blur also injected the spirit of Ray Davies into their music, Oasis were more indebted to Jagger and Richards. Nevertheless, Blur and Oasis seemed of a breed: tributaries flowing from a shared source and then later into a common delta we lazily dubbed Britpop.

Until the singles war of 1995, you were allowed to love both too – the later friction between art-school bourgeois and northern working class was not so apparent. It is now obvious that these were always completely incompatible groups, so opposed in both essence and existence, belonging to entirely different schools of pop art. But for most of 1994, they could be happily yoked together as the Best of British, as harbingers of a new pop order and a nation's renaissance. The civil war would have to wait.

The Burnage days were coming to an end. Noel and Guigs had already gone; Creation had slated 'Supersonic' for an April release; it could not be long before the nation at large took the rest of the group away from Manchester. But then, they'd hardly been local scene heroes for long, certainly not compared to the Roses, New Order and Mondays. Most observers place the true beginning of the Oasis buzz at around May 1993. They'd barely had time to enjoy an elevated local status, even if they'd wanted to; Guigs and Noel were on the train to London before they could reach street-recognition stage. Compared to the Roses' epic five years around Manchester before Spike Island, it was a period of indecent brevity. Perhaps this explains why they are not cherished and adored by their own city as much as some of their forebears were, not even by those who know nothing of Oasis's ambivalence towards Manchester. Oasis are a Mancunian band, but they were never quite *The* Manchester Band. Anyone who saw the Stone Roses at the Apollo during Xmas '95 knows who still held that title – as the crowd sang that night, 'You're the pride of Manchester.'

Mid-March 1994. Liam's back in town, in between gigs, still hanging out with the boys. Liam, the Shenton brothers and Chris are all watching football on the telly when Liam, casually, pipes up: 'The single's out next month. And I think we're gonna be on the cover of the *NME*.' There's a sense of unreality about it all. Chris chips in: 'Get us some signed copies, Will – they might be worth something one day.' And he thinks: 'Well, yeah, they might be, mightn't they?' He never got the records, naturally. Instead, Liam walked away that day with £20-worth of Roses rarities, promising to pay up next time he saw the lads. Which he never did.

A week later, Oasis performed on *The Word*, thanks to a leg-up from the much-maligned but under-estimated Terry Christian. The power of the media in deciding what a nation should consume was definitively demonstrated: Oasis gig attendances trebled overnight, and the press came banging on the door. Nothing had changed in Oasis's nature, only the perception of it.

Chris's perception, watching at home, was that it still felt surreal. He knew those guys on the screen intimately, yet it didn't feel connected to him, sat in Burnage. Only on April 18 did it hit home. The single had been out since Monday and the mid-week positions suggested it might actually chart first time. The lads, including Liam, were playing Sunday football as usual, the one constant in a rapidly changing world. Suddenly Liam stopped, shouted 'I'm off to listen to the charts' and disappeared. For good, as it turned out.

Chris went home and heard the record go in at 31. Now it connected. And *how*.

*   *   *

In June 1994, just before the release of 'Shakermaker', Oasis finally came home to a gig of a size befitting their new status. About a thousand curious Mancunians swarmed into Manchester University hall, the vast majority seeing the band for the first time. As Paul Gallagher later implied, this could easily have been a disaster had not Oasis performed so well. Those in the audience who'd been muttering about the band not paying their local dues would've pounced. Still, the sceptics were easily outnumbered by recent converts who'd seen *The Word*, bought 'Supersonic' and heard 'Shakermaker' getting the Radio One pre-release treatment. When a new arrival to the national stage hears the words of its singles and B-sides being sung straight back at them, they know they're on the fast-track to the top.

Chris had laughed his head off when he first heard the new single: surely they were not going to get away with ripping off a bloody Coca-cola jingle?! But, like most people, he knew a Top 20 hit when he heard one. And for the first time, he felt an unexpected tremor of pride. After all, he'd played a significant part in the Oasis story – that was the band he'd put together up on the *Chart Show* screen. Why not go to the gig, as the rest of town was doing? Why not the post-gig party too? He had more right than most of the assorted hangers-on and music-biz vultures to be there, right?

Outside the university, he managed to get a call put through to Liam's mobile phone in the dressing room.

'All right, Will, it's Chrissy H: can you get us into the gig?'

'No chance, mate, you're fuckin' trippin'.'

'Well, give us a word with Guigsy then.'

(Amidst the background noise, he could hear his old best mate talking to Liam: 'Fuck off, I don't wanna talk to him.')

Liam came back onto the line: 'Sorry mate, Guigs can't do anything for you. See ya.'

Chris: 'Okay, what about Tony Mac then?'

Liam: 'What the fuck can he do? He's only the fucking drummer.'

At that moment, Mark Shenton, Liam's old best mate, sauntered over to Chris: 'Here y'are, Chris, I've got a spare place on my guest pass. Bunk in with me mate.'

Emboldened by several pints and the good-time vibe, Chris made his way over to the back-stage entrance as the lights came up after the finale. An array of monkeys in suits barred the way – big-time security already, it seemed. Just at that moment, Liam popped into view over the bouncers' shoulders: 'S'all right lads, let 'em in, they're with us.' A pang of guilt, perhaps? Liam swiftly apologized for the earlier conversation: 'It was out of my control, mate. Enjoy yourself.'

In the corner, surrounded by former Oasis patrons the Real People, sat Guigsy. Clapping eyes on Chris, he looked stunned. Chris resolved to keep his cool – there'd be no showing-up here if he could help it. Breezing over, he chatted amiably to Guigs, who visibly relaxed when he realized Chris wasn't going to

gob him. Strangely, it turned into the best chat they'd
had since the split; both achieved some sort of release.

After half an hour, Guigs beckoned Chris over to the
bogs. Crouching in a cubicle, Guigs laid out four lines
of coke which the two snorted through a rolled-up
tenner. The classic rock-star scene, then, and Chris
felt the symbolism immediately: no more toking on
small-time weed in Erwood Park from now on – it'd
be bank-notes and powder all the way for Guigs.

'Come back to the house – we'll do a few more lines,'
exhorted Guigs. But this wasn't Chris's universe and it
never would be. The charlie-class don't live in Burnage
and work in a factory. Chris made his excuses and left
to go to a party downstairs. 'All right,' conceded Guigs,
'but come round tomorrow anyway – I'll give you a
copy of the album we're puttin' out. I'm tellin' ya, it's
an unbelievable record.'

Chris called round next morning. Guigs opened
the door; he'd never seen him look so drained or
hammered. 'Oh, right, hang on – I'll get the tape.'
Chris stood open-mouthed as Guigs left him on the
doorstep, shutting the door in his face as he went off to
ferret about upstairs. So much for the apparent *détente*
thought Chris; perhaps it had been the coke talking.
Finally, he returned, thrusting a run-off from the master copy into Chris's hand. *Definitely Maybe* read the cassette spine. Another awkward silence, 1991 vintage.

'So, er, when's yer next gig then?'

'Glastonbury.'

'No, I mean round here.'

223 ■

'Oh. Er, the Haçienda.'
'Right. Can you sort me for the guest list?'
'Yeah, no problem.'
'Nice one. I'll get off then.'
'Yeah, see ya.'
Needless to say, Chris's name was not included on the Haçienda guest list and Chris never saw Guigsy face-to-face again.

One consolation from the evening for Chris had been the chance to doss about with the Real People. The Real People's most famous contribution to Oasis's career was their generosity in recording Noel's band on their eight-track gear, producing the first definitive Oasis demo.

Less well-known is that singer Tony Griffiths spent a lot of time helping Liam get his vocal techniques sorted, introducing him to the science of tone production and projection. It has been a recurrent problem that, because Liam never had formal instruction of the sort Chris received in choir, he has never 'sung properly', overloading his throat by under-using his diaphragm. Eventually such abuse leads to complete loss of voice. More recently, Liam apparently took some instruction from a well-known female voice coach in Didsbury. Those who criticize Liam for his narrow stylistic range will have to wait and see if he can expand as he learns how to control his voice 'professionally'.

Sadly for the scousers, whose music always sat very

snugly next to Oasis's, they were lost in the stampede as Oasis broke big, leading some ignorant punters to remark that they were Oasis-copyists when they re-emerged with a new album in 1996. Such public perceptions can be fatal. It was reminiscent of the brilliant Pretty Things' fate when they took *SF Sorrow* to the States, only to be accused of plagiarising the Who's *Tommy*, despite Townshend's admission that he'd been inspired by their album (which was released two years earlier in the UK). The Real People have taken it all remarkably well. Indeed, Liverpool in general has embraced Oasis even more than Manchester has, indicating that Oasis sit even better in the Scousepop lineage than they do in Manchester's less melody-driven tradition. The Las' Lee Mavers, whose masterwork was actually recorded in 1987 and seems like a template for Oasis's debut, noticed this too. When he met Noel years later, Gallagher remarked how chuffed he was to meet him: 'Yeah, I bet you are,' smirked Mavers, secure in the knowledge that he had first claim on Britpop.

Tony Wilson always argued that the spirit of the Beatles dominated Liverpool in a way that it didn't in Manchester, producing Scousepop bands who revelled in pure melody and harmonies; while Mancs preferred less chirpy, more rhythmically-centred music. In brief: the Happy Mondays could not have emerged from Liverpool; equally, Cast could never have developed in Manchester. It is no surprise that Oasis's most devoted adherents amidst their peers, Smaller and the Real People, are Scouse not Manc. I've heard many

Liverpudlians remark that Oasis always sound like they should've come from Liverpool not Manchester.

The entire nation is well aware of the viciousness of the Manc–Scouse rivalry, most notoriously expressed through football aggro down the years between United and Liverpool. Economically and politically too: the Manchester runway affair may now have been hijacked by Swampy and his pals but for years it was a battle-ground for Liverpool's and Manchester's civic and business leaders to seek regional economic supremacy. Left-wingers in each city carped at each other throughout the eighties as Liverpool took the Militant route whilst Manchester and Graham Stringer became proto-Blairites.

Chris, like most United fans, has had a jaundiced view of the Scousers down the years but, as Bod Gallagher rightly argued in his book, music is the one area which allows a cessation of hostilities. The competition between the two cities is friendlier, more supportive, with bands such as the Roses and Bunnymen being welcomed the other side of the East Lancs Road with open arms – producing a cross-fertilization which only strengthens the north-west's position as the cockpit of English pop. Oasis, in some ways, are the inevitable result: a nominally Mancunian band who seem to be as much influenced by, and more appreciated amongst, Scousers.

18

Stop Me If You Think You've Heard This One Before

What is it about Oasis that has taken them to such a level of success? It is not good enough for the fan simply to declare that their inherent brilliance is the answer – pop history is littered with great artists whose records never broke the Top 40. A historian might introduce the oldest debate in the book at this point, that which spins around the 'Great Man' theory of history. Essentially, you can lay out two extremes of position. One argues that certain historical actors intervene with such charisma and personal force that they shape and alter the social, economic and political tides by their individual actions. The other view proclaims such forces to be unstoppable; major historical actors are merely agents driven by these forces who succeed only because they adapt to them. So, for example, Hitler is seen by the former school of thought as such a world-changing force that, had he been killed at birth, neither Nazism nor World War Two would have occurred. The other would claim that German history and ideology, the Versailles Treaty and the crash of 1929 combined to make the events of 1933-45 inevitable; another figure would eventually have been produced by these forces to play the Hitler role.

Normally, the truth is somewhere between the two, though most historians tend to lean their conclusions towards the inevitable force theorem. So too with Oasis: they had a set of attributes unmatched by their contemporaries which dovetailed exactly with the demands of the historical moment. Three years earlier or later and their arrival on the scene might have been completely inappropriate.

So: Oasis placed The Song at the heart of their project, exactly at the moment when Blur and Suede had demonstrated the public's thirst for the return of the radio-friendly guitar-based 'classic' tune. Indeed, they took it further, developing by 1995 into an organ- ization which could reach out to groups of the popula- tion Blur and Suede did not seek. 'Don't Look Back In Anger' is the apex of this: a middle of the road anthem sung by grannies and children, teachers and pupils, Brits and foreigners – in short, Oasis became the first band Everyman could like since you-know-who.

Tunes that are honed to reach out in such a way speak of the larger philosophy behind the group. We live in an increasingly atomized culture in which every possible sub-sect of interest is catered for. We no longer all sit around the telly and watch the same programmes, or listen en masse to the Top 40, or call ourselves C of E. And although we must welcome this, for our individual demands have created this world, we do still seem to crave some shared reference points, some experiences that remind us we're a nation. Any cultural phenomenon that promises inclusivity, preferably laced with positivity, is seized upon by a grateful public, keen to find something we can all relate to and talk about to each other. Euro '96 did it; *Eastenders* just about qualifies; and surely this is what Oasis have now achieved as well. A judge could once ask 'What is Gazza?' and keep his job; were he to demand 'Who is Liam Gallagher?' today, the press would howl for his dismissal, and quite rightly. Being able to hum the opening bars of 'Wonderwall' is as good a test as any that you've been resident in Britain for these last two years.

Naturally, there are other features of Oasis which chime with the times and which cement their relationship with the public. The rise of the Lad, as exemplified by *Loaded* magazine and its thousand derivatives across the media, has created a nurturing environment for a swaggering, brass-necked outfit like Oasis. Indeed, Noel specifically welcomes the association, often telling *Loaded* hacks that he'd love to present a 'Loaded TV' show from his front room. Linked to this is the nineties mania for sensual hedonism, replacing the rampant materialism of the eighties, which the drug-fuelled songs of Oasis soundtrack perfectly. This decade is also marked by its guilt-free apolitical nature, whereby it has never been trendier to say that you have no

229 ∎

interest in political ideas or the state of the nation, unless it impacts directly upon your own hedonism. Oasis's non-political stance – calling for a vote for Blairite mush clearly doesn't count – combined with the odd shout in favour of drugs fits our current ethos precisely.

Tightening the focus even more sharply, it appears Oasis fulfilled longstanding demands within the committed music audience too. Guitar-based indie groups used to flaunt their shambling amateurism and uncompromising anti-commercialism to the fans' approval. But by the turn of the decade, such attitudes had become stale and hackneyed. The fastest route to vilification now was to come out with the classic indie saddo line: 'We make records for ourselves and if anyone else likes them, it's a bonus.' Madchester had proved that commercial success need not have an inversely proportional relationship to artistic credibility. Furthermore, the sonic sophistication of many Madchester records had exposed many of the crappy mid-eighties guitar bands for the talentless chancers that they were. Good production and performances were revealed not necessarily to be the imprint of The Man's malevolence but signs of artists who cared about their music and mission. And tunelessness was no longer an ideologically sound badge declaring one's opposition to chart-pop's banalities but a simple indication that you couldn't write a proper melody to save your life.

Oasis and their contemporaries have responded to

this by making indie mainstream, by re-establishing the beat group line-up and by releasing songs written on guitars rather than tracks on sequencers. To some, this development which gave birth to Britpop was a disaster, the death of 'progress'; to others, it was a merciful release from the deadly pincer movement of US rock and UK dance. It is probably regrettable that the subsequent three years have witnessed the fast-forward replay of the history of British pop: from Dad-rock's 1965 pastiches, to Kula Shaker's 1967 reprise and now onto prog-rock and beyond with Mansun and Radiohead. Half-a-dozen excellent albums have resulted, but what does it signify for pop's future? As Stephen Dalton asked Peter Hook recently, doesn't it dishearten you that nobody seems to have picked up the modernist baton from Joy Division and New Order?

The one record collection that matters above all others to Oasis is, of course, the Beatles canon. Comparisons in the press between the bands, mainly fatuous and gro-tesque, are none the less inevitable. The scale of Oasis's sales, the Everyman appeal and inclusivity both bands shared and the obvious musical similarities demand that Oasis be measured against the Fab Four's benchmark. Noel knows this more than most, though his response has been wildly variable, veering from outright ven-eration to charmless boasts such as 'Our first two albums are better than anyone else's, including the Beatles'.' That is perhaps a reflection on the unfairness of dragging him into such a fruitless and dangerous debate – and one which he can only lose, whatever the criteria – but he does seem to ask for trouble sometimes. Try this, from Hewitt's book: 'When we play to ETs on Mars, I'll tell them, "Look, you're going to hear about the Beatles but don't take any notice. They were all right – but Oasis, that's the ones you want."' Nurse! The screens! And the gobshite antidote!

As for Oasis's habit of co-opting Beatlisms, it could be argued that they would be an even better group if they did so more assiduously; it's best to make sure that the group they're worshipping is actually the one that existed. It does sometimes appear that Noel and Liam's hazy perceptions, especially about Lennon, are testament to their late arrival at the Beatles shrine. The infamous and hilarious taped barney between the Gallaghers as to who had the greater claim to Lennon's soul manages to hearten and dismay simultaneously. For despite Goldman, despite Yoko, despite *Double Fantasy*, Lennon's mantle has remained a prize for each successive musical generation to fight over.

Undoubtedly, Liam *is* the closest thing to Lennon in Oasis. The instinctive spontaneity, genuinely rebellious anti-Establishment impulse and reckless willingness to place art above comfort or expediency are pure Lennon. But within a breath, Liam is away on his trademark anti-student, anti-bourgeois, anti-intellectualism rant. If he is, as he claims, the reincarnated Beatle, then somewhere during an obviously traumatic rebirth, he's forgotten the resolutely lower-middle-class semi, the Liverpool Art Institute and the 300 books a year he had Mal Evans buy for him. There is no doubting Liam's love of Lennon but it's a partial, misunderstood passion at best. Only those addicted to the historic pick 'n' mix could so flamboyantly parade in a hero's garb, having failed to recognize its noblest features.

Perhaps this is the inevitable result of not reading a book in your life: if Liam has only relied on the primal scream in Lennon's voice and the flickering images from *Anthology* for his image of John, then it's understandable that the essence of the man has escaped him. But why Noel should want to argue over this hazy Lennon legacy is a mystery, unless it's to help hide the truth. For big brother is the closest thing we have to a Paul McCartney for the nineties. It isn't the fact that Noel and Liam are brothers which makes Oasis 'work' but that their synergy replicates that of John and Paul. And this is apparently not something Noel wishes to admit or accept. He's smart enough to know that lip-service to 'The Rebel' or Lennon-figure is mandatory – McCartneyesque cautious innovation and *realpolitik* is the love that dare not speak its name. (That an identification with Paul, whether by self or by others, should be a source of embarrassment is a sad reflection on history's treatment of McCartney. Without him, the post-66 Beatles would've sunk into grotesque self-indulgence and posturing, not to mention probable indolence.)

That Oasis have borrowed some chord and melody patterns from the Fabs is obvious. That they also place The Song above all other considerations equally so. The latter clearly does them more credit than the former. But most of the other colours in the Beatles' palate are left untouched. A little more careful derivation could be welcome. One aspect Noel has taken on board, to a larger extent than may be wise, is the anthem. Noel would later repeat, almost word for word, Lennon's remark that he loved to hear his more anthemic songs sung by football crowds, in pubs or at demonstrations. Lennon added in 1972 that he would henceforth like to write such songs for 'the revolution' (hence 'Power To The People').

It's an understandable goal but one that too easily produces lowest common denominator music. Most Beatle-written anthems were either never that highly regarded to start with or dated badly as their inherent musical weakness became grating (see 'All You Need Is Love', 'Yellow Sub', 'Give Peace A Chance'). Anthems, virtually by definition, must be almost moronically simplistic, easily roared by an off-key crowd, as catchy as an ad jingle – you can end up with 'Sailing' if you're not careful. Rare are those anthems which endure like 'Hey Jude', which is one reason why the Beatles actually wrote so few of them, preferring quirky miniatures or subtle growers as they progressed.

Noel gives the impression of trying to write every other song as an anthem, inspired as he is by Kippax memories, lessons learned from house tunes at the Haç and simple Irish singalongs from his childhood. Only 'Don't Look Back In Anger' promises to endure like 'Hey Jude', although 'Wonderwall' is admittedly taking a long time to jade despite the monotony of its chorus. It is a healthy ambition to want the Beatles' popular touch, but without due care a popular touch can become banal populism.

The Beatles never made that slip, largely because the writers shared a crucial experience so often lambasted by Oasis – an art school/student background which gave them an experimental, challenging edge and a necessary tinge of elitist drive. The irony is that the Beatles as individuals resemble Blur more than Oasis (and Blur do a better Fab-power song, 'Beetlebum'). The stylistic range, dedication to reinvention and the senses of ironic distance and playfulness the Beatles displayed are foreign to Oasis, but typical of any art-school band. Instead of sneering at bourgeois arty pretension, Oasis should look at any random roll-call of the student class they Paul Calfishly despise: the Beatles, Jagger 'n' Richards, Ray Davies, Townshend, Roxy Music, the Pistols . . . need we continue? Oasis will have to learn to live with the swots – and maybe crib an equation or two.

19

Death At One's Elbow

If Chris ever felt isolated as a 'victim' of Oasis, left by the wayside, then he only had to wait until March 1995 for some company – Tony McCarroll. The persecution endured by Tony is well documented in Ian Robertson's book, a tale from which only Bonehead emerges with any credit at all, as he occasionally tried to shield Tony from the others' invective. One cannot help chuckling at the lack of irony in Liam's and Guigsy's comments about Tony, as reported to Paolo Hewitt. Liam, not a favourite for any rocket scientist diploma, accused Tony of 'being too thick'; Guigsy picked on Tony's alleged lack of instrumental progress, hardly from the vantage point of world's greatest bassist. Yet the eventual break appears to have been as much of a surprise to Tony as the 1991 coup had to Chris. On a football field complex in Gorton, about four days after the first reports that Tony had been sacked, Chris spotted him on the pitch next to his.

'Tony, what happened?'

'I don't really know, I don't know what's going on.'

'They're saying you're out . . .'

'Yeah, they just said "You're not in the band any-more" and put the phone down.'

'Who did, Noel?'

'No. He got Marcus Russell [*Oasis's manager*] to do it. None of the band spoke to me.' Tony still looked shell-shocked and as though he thought it might all turn out to have been a ghastly mistake. But it wasn't. A month later, Chris met Tony again for an update.

'So, what's going on?'

'Well, solicitors are involved now. I can't talk to the press or anything either.'

'Have the band talked to you?'

'Not really. Just Bonehead – he phoned to see how I was, like he was making sure I was all right.'

Tony shrugged his shoulders and remarked that the atmosphere within the band had been shit anyway. Noel was hanging out with Weller all the time or househunting. Yet Tony was being told that he wasn't sufficiently into being part of the band's social whirl, which was partially true – he liked to come home, see his mates, hang out in Levenshulme and play football. He looked after his roots, which apparently counted against him. Tony made no mention of his drumming being an issue, however. Later, the official Oasis books would lambast him for his supposed technical shortcomings.

Whatever reasons existed for Tony's apparent un-
suitability, it still seemed to Chris and everyone else
in Burnage that he had been treated quite shittily.
In Chris's opinion Tony was, and remains, a nice,
genuine bloke. As we've seen, it appears you need
to be a bastard to get on in this business.

(It occurred to Chris that messy, ignoble departures
were becoming a pattern with Oasis. Joining Tony and
himself in the dumpster was Tony French, the designer
who thought of and executed the swirl logo. He only
found out that his services were no longer welcome
when he overheard someone telling another gig-goer
at the Newcastle Verve/Oasis show that Brian Cannon
would be the designer in future. At the time Tony was
gutted of course, doubly so when he realized how
ridiculously cheaply he had sold his own rights in
the logo. Days after he sold out to Oasis for £3,000,
two members of Manchester's touting fraternity told
him he'd fucked up: they'd have had bags round his
house containing 15 grand in cash within the hour if
he'd sold to them. Doh!)

Chris was particularly interested to hear how Guigsy
was getting on. At one point during the previous few
months, he'd clearly been fretting about the future,
telling Tony, 'Me and you have got to sort ourselves
out and get it together, or else we're out of this band.'
Somehow Guigs had survived, yet again, whilst a
comrade fell away. Tony painted a graphic picture
of a severely unbalanced Guigs–Noel relationship.
(Within a week Chris was also hearing strange and

unprintable rumours around Burnage about how the first album was recorded.)

Before Christmas, Noel had told an interviewer that Oasis was indivisible: 'If our drummer left, that would be the end of Oasis.' Yet, as has become clear, some in the band had been angling to get rid of Tony from the moment they signed to Creation. The reason they didn't was that it would've set them back in the race to the top. Not for too long, but certainly for a few months as they found and bedded-in a new drummer. There is a brutal pragmatism about the way Tony was kept in the band on sufferance and then jettisoned when the recording of *Morning Glory* was due to begin. Far cleaner to get it straight from the start – but that would've cost time and money. Worse, Oasis had lived for months off the media image that they were a real 'gang' band, all lads together in a tight, local unit taking on the world. You can understand and even appreciate all the band's methodology and reasoning behind the McCarroll treatment – but it's impossible to admire.

Alan White, Tony's successor, is the brother of perhaps the best drummer in British pop, Steve White, who gives Weller's band a surging dynamism. You could argue that his introduction, with his supposed superior range and skill, is an obvious sign of Noel's ambition, proof that he's understood his band needs to extend its narrow rhythmical range. Unfortunately, there was virtually no evidence of that on *Morning Glory*, all of which McCarroll could surely have performed quite well enough. The medium, four-square tempo of most Oasis material pre-1997 never required much more than power and good time-keeping, which Tony Mac didn't lack.

Noel has argued, through Hewitt, that a technically proficient drummer will allow him to expand the group's musical vocabulary by opening up new rhythmic possibilities. The implication was that he could have written more interesting material, exploring band dynamics and rhythmic variations, if he had felt that the drummer was up to it. The third album (not released at the time of writing) should have illustrated if this was the case, or whether he was blaming Tony Mac's alleged deficiencies in order to mask his own compositional limitations.

In any event, as anyone who's been in a band will tell you, it is hard to produce fully satisfying band music – as opposed to simply arranging a writer's songs – if the band members are not involved in the writing or arranging themselves at an early point in the creative process. Go watch Godard's film of the Stones working out 'Sympathy For The Devil' virtually from scratch to see how a classic song also becomes a classic record and a classic performance.

Maybe Noel should get the benefit of the doubt. Some critics would argue that being brought up on the meat 'n' potato square rhythms of white rock left Noel bereft of rhythmic vision. Hewitt noted that he'd not heard important black artists such as Sly Stone until he moved to London and met Weller. Since it is black musical influence that gives superior pop and rock its sex, funkiness and movement, it is not surprising that Oasis sound plodding compared to the pulsing rhythmic interplay in some Mondays and Roses music. One hopes he's been listening to the right records in Weller's collection and taking advantage of Alan White's capabilities to influence the base of the third album. If it was, as Noel perhaps facetiously replied to queries, 'more of the same pub-rock bollocks', then McCarroll's overthrow was in vain. We hope he was joking.

20

You Just Haven't Earned It Yet, Baby

Very early on in Oasis's career – before even their first single had been released – it became a commonplace in the British music press to suggest that Oasis would, at last, regain the colonies for us. The United States of America, still music's biggest and most lucrative market, had remained largely immune to the charms of British music since the bizarre and ridiculous New Pop invasion of the early eighties. (Perhaps therein lies the reason: could we expect them to forgive us after inflicting Duran Duran upon them?) We often affect not to be bothered by this failure; we proclaim, 'We are the best and fuck the world for being so stupid.'

Unfortunately for the chauvinists, the bands themselves don't buy it. They all lust after America's markets and the guaranteed entry into the rest of the world's. More than that, US success brings both kudos and security. To be the Brit band that cracks the States guarantees dribbling adoration from the entire nation, a knockout blow against your puny domestic rivals and protection against the notorious fickleness of the British.

Indeed, it is under the latter rainbow that the biggest pot of gold lies. An artist can disappear off the British commercial and critical radar completely in the space of just one album; to return from such a blow in this country is almost impossible. Loserhood is permanent. You can think of a dozen such afflicted bands straight off can't you? Once you've made the top in the States, however, two American syndromes make a difference. First, you don't have to cope with the carping, challenging, build-em-up-knock-em-down brigade; success and its creators are venerated in the States, not stalked (at least not figuratively, anyway). Second, falling off a log in the States is an incredibly tricky business. The flipside of progress being so slow is that regression can be just as time-consuming, much to the delight of the artist.

Declines in chart sales and reputations are gentle in the States – McCartney's took almost 15 post-Beatle years to reach near rock-bottom; Dylan's is still slithering. New York may have decided you're finished, but you'll still be big in Tucson, Arizona for a while yet. And the Americans love a bounce-back; follow the Difficult Second Album's commercial suicide with a half-decent, hard-working third and they'll love you for it instead of ridiculing your persistence. For the artist looking to keep a career floating until retirement/heroin overdose, America is Valhalla.

All right: to be less cynical, there is also the business of immortality. If you go into a band seeking to join the Beatles, Stones, Hendrix *et al.* in the Hall of Fame, you need the States' approval, whether it be commercial or critical. You cannot expect to be worshipped in history by the world if your success has been confined to these tiny islands. Oasis, more aware than most of rock's history and their place within it, know that to be mentioned by others seriously in the same breath as the Beatles necessitates a rampant conquest of the States.

Oasis know all this. There's been some trendy bitching from the band about America but they've worked the circuits hard and tried to play the game, with Noel in particular eager not to cause offence. They don't always get it right, of course. Liam's display of gobbing in New York might have played well to London's sillier circles but not to Manhattanites. Cynics often suggest that Oasis's music has seemingly been designed to appeal to Americans above all else: blue-collar but safe, genuine rather than ironic, loud but not nasty guitars, anthemically sing-song without being blatant pop mush and so on. Indeed, those Brits who still resist the band often cite these built-for-US mechanics as a major reason for disliking them, hearing too many echoes of Springsteen or Neil Young for comfort. Above all, Oasis are resolutely a live act – the necessary condition of US rock audience-building – and can give 'professional' performances, sounding close to the recorded product. This is what heartland America demands – Oasis will sock it to 'em, pardner.

At the absolute zenith of their popularity in the UK, during the winter of 1995–96, Oasis played a series of shows in the States. Conventional wisdom had it that the Americans wouldn't be able to resist our conquering heroes for much longer. After all, this time we were sending over something clearly tailor-made for their MidWest audiences and po-faced critical establishment; instead of taking the piss by despatching the hopelessly English Suede and Blur.

Yet still the Yanks responded with a shrugged 'So what?' From the public, the message seemed to be 'You just haven't earned it yet, baby', which the band and its management were at least half-expecting. They had always been prepared for the long, multi-toured haul. But the critical response was more of a surprise. There is a long tradition of US critics being suspicious of UK favourites, since we have picked up a damaging reputation as a nation which uncritically hypes those who do not deserve it and who later collapse in ignominy (usually on a Tap-esque US tour).

This is related to our love of pop ephemera, to our devotion to the utterly new and playful, to the concept that only the very young can carry new pop's seed. We benefit from what seems to be a vibrant, ever-changing, multi-coloured pop scene and snigger at the lumbering, slow-developing US equivalent. Chart movement was always a good indicator of this supposed cultural difference, as new acts race up and down ours in three weeks flat while US singles crawl over a period of months around Billboard's 100 (which demands several attempts from newcomers before they're even allowed to enter).

But for the best of the American critics, this wasn't a factor with Oasis. Self-evidently, Oasis were a cut above the normal Brit exports, unlikely to be derided in the MidWest for not being able to play properly, for lack of rockin' stamina or for over-use of eyeliner. No, the supposed problem with Oasis was the void alleged to exist at their core. A pop act like the Spice Girls – *pace* their absurd girlpower manifesto – can get away with vapidity, but a self-proclaimed rock act, coming to the home of Real Rock, cannot. Perhaps the greatest of modern American critics, Dave Marsh wrote most tellingly on the issue for *Mojo* magazine:

'In all my life, I've never seen a show more dramatically dead, more devoted to the projection of mannerism rather than – almost in spite of – personality; a show so shorn of the volatility that has made rock'n'roll thrilling since Little Richard and Elvis. What's most striking about this bland-ness, dullness and chipper arrogance is the degree to which it is completely and utterly calculated. Oasis seem to have a very recondite and elaborate theory of how rock 'ought' to work. In a way, it's the punk aesthetic turned back-to-back, a music in which context has been so far subordinated to form that there's an active hostility to making a point . . . Oasis manage to take the riotous teen anthems of yesteryear and remove from them all aspects of riot, without which an anthem – at least a rock anthem – hasn't much point or purpose. What's left is a form of entertainment so polished and sterile it's as easy to admire as the Crown Jewels. Unfortunately, it's equally hard to touch.

The parts of the audience looking for depth – emotional depth, lyrical depth, depth of ideas about things other than music – will almost certainly have to move beyond Oasis. Or maybe the world has changed far more than I imagine, in which case their success portends a new era for music and for youth culture in general. It may well be that what Oasis' audience loves about the group is precisely their lack of emotion, their distance, their superficiality. If that's the case, it symbolizes a genuinely revolutionary change. Not only The Beatles, but every important band that arose in their wake, represented some basic philosophical idea. More than that, declaring yourself a fan of that band meant staking out a position in defence of that idea. Oasis represent a principle . . . not hermeticism or narcissism, or even art for art's sake, but defeatism. The Gallaghers have chosen to distance themselves from emotion, to obliterate interaction among band members or with the audience in order to make a point about what is possible – or rather, what is not. [Hundreds of bands] believed that their music could change the world, or at least the part of the world with which they came face to face.

Oasis overtly declare that this is a ludicrous, impossible goal. The world will not change: you might, but that's nothing more than a detail . . .

In this respect, Oasis may not find their audience quite so irrelevant. They need the worship of their fans to authenticate their right to stand where they do. Gaining the top of the charts is the certification of maximum achievement. If Oasis manage to sustain this career, that means that this idea has prevailed, that it has penetrated deep into the collective consciousness of mass culture.'

Oasis had finally received in the States the sort of examination we Brits had excused them, coming back with report cards stamped 'D-plus, must try harder'. And no doubt they will, for Oasis will surely not concede defeat – they were built to be America's chosen Limeys.

But that is the critical response; and America has always taken rock criticism incredibly seriously, prompting many Brits to accuse them of pomposity and an over-zealous pursuit of 'worthiness'. Oasis show no signs of caring what the Yank elite think – their concerns are for the ticket-buying punters, who pay even less attention to what the critics write than Brit audiences do. America, weirdly, thus boasts the most erudite critical elite in the world and – judging by its charts – the most tasteless consumers. Alan McGhee, Oasis's label boss, has no doubts about the inevitability of Oasis conquering the States, despite the critical flak.

As he told Sean O'Hagan: 'Oasis are going to be up there with U2. We're talking at least ten million US sales of the next record. Nobody since Led Zep has done what Oasis have done – taken British pop culture and sold it to the Americans.' If that means holding their collective noses to share an LA stage with Blur, or accepting a support slot to U2, or playing the MTV video game, so be it. Many years ago, bands like the Smiths and Stone Roses used to reject mega-group support slots as being beneath them: independent purity mattered more to them than breaking the States. The Smiths would never have stood a chance anyway with their self-sacrificial aversion to videos. Oasis have learned that you must compromise to succeed globally, that rave notices from Anglophile US critics are worthless unless you try to sell the local public what they want. This is not a criticism but a simple recognition of Oasis's *realpolitik*: this is a band committed to commercial success above all else. They will break America within the next two years whether the critics come round to them or not. What price an Oasis re-enactment of Shea Stadium by next Christmas? Odds-on, surely – certainly, shorter odds than the Roses were ever offered Stateside.

21

Oscillate Wildly

The Stone Roses by Mick Middles

Slowly came the Roses. Very slowly. Edging out of a deadening fog, often mistakenly referred to as 'Goth'. But, if their early influences were clumsy, if they clashed too heavily on stage and on demo, they weren't necessarily so obvious. The parochial mid-eighties music of the Stone Roses would be a place to locate, perhaps, the Seeds, Roger McGuinn. It was Lydon and Pop rather than Eldritch and Jim Morrison. Nevertheless, for quite a while, they did seem to be held in an unattractive, unfashionable glue of sound, and perhaps mercifully, for half a decade they failed to emerge into any kind of serious spotlight. (Not through lack of trying. Outraged Manchester news stories would tell of a prominent Stone Roses graffito on the city's proud Central Library ... and then another on the severe grey exterior of Queen Victoria, and then another ... 'We didn't do it,' screamed the band. 'We know who did, but we are not telling.'

251 ∎

One recalls a Haçienda Roses gig in mid-'85, when 150 Roses 'friends' gathered on that soon-to-be-famous dance-floor: a sullen, sexless, pint-clutching rabble. Flashes of paisley and grimy denim, rock-length hair and even – I swear – studded belts. A vague sixties feel, late to be re-inserted into the fashion swirl but, back then, in the smart, cold, grey, angular Haçienda – a place normally punched along by New Order, latter-day electro and embryonic 'House' – it all seemed so hopelessly passé. Haçienda regulars, such as they were, were neat little kids then, famously linked, or so we liked to think, with the cutting-edge clubbers of New York, where smart street-style and dance-chic had blown away the denim residue of rock – we thought – for ever. But here, before the eyes of a trickle of unimpressed A&R men, the Stone Roses seemed jammed firmly into retro. We assumed a condescending air, and smiled and, possibly, even clapped at the death. But we knew – or we thought we knew – better!

The Stone Roses were conceived, one might reasonably presume, on the day when Ian Brown met John Squire. Two curiously aloof 11-year-olds, already searching for something beyond the norm. Six years later, their friendship etched in stone (or maybe not, as it would turn out), they had formed their first band: a ramshackle affair named the Patrol who, fuelled by the lingering spirit of the Pistols and the Clash, added a certain spark to youth club discos of Sale in 1981. By this time, with any chance of academia already hastily jettisoned, Squire had been fortunate enough to find a job – constructing models for an animation company – that encouraged his artistic leanings.

Brown, by comparison, had opted for Kerouacian romance,

hitchhiking across Europe, serving time as a building-site labourer, or washing dishes, or office dogsbody; anything to keep his pink Lambretta burning away at the rear of a locally notorious Sale scooter gang. It would take four years for the Patrol to slowly mutate into the Stone Roses – a strong name famously gleaned from the cover of a ratty fifties paperback pulp thriller that Brown found lurking in a dustbin. (And better, too, than the dreadful, though not entirely inappropriate, moniker they almost adopted: 'The Angry Young Teddy Bears'.)

As 1985 dawned, the Stone Roses immediately, and as it would turn out perceptively, distanced themselves from a Manchester band scene still sagging beneath the weight of countless dreary Smiths copyists, who had metamorphosed, rather pointlessly, from countless dreary Joy Division copyists. Although, with Simply Red, James, Easterhouse, Happy Mondays *et al.* on the horizon, the greying, raincoated, short back'n'sides archetype of a Manchester band still remained in place. The Stone Roses' first single, initially entitled 'Misery Dictionary', was an attempt to lampoon that image, to evoke a vivacious, colourful, arrogantly un-Mancunian stance. Unsure of whether public or press would see the joke, the band opted for the more obvious title, 'So Young'.

'All our songs are totally optimistic,' Brown significantly noted, in his very first press interview (with Manchester's lost glossy *Muze* magazine).

Cleverly, the Stone Roses generally side-stepped the deadening local band circuit and opted, instead, to perform at a short series of secretly arranged 'warehouse parties' when, as if a romantic precursor to the rave scene, their trickle of followers would be guided to undisclosed venues. Their mystique gained momentum with gigging sojourns to unknown outposts in Sweden or, more bizarrely perhaps, Preston. By August '85, as Manchester's rediscovered thirst for live music was satisfied by the aforementioned hopefuls and a curiously open-minded booking policy at the International venue, the Roses remained noticeably aloof, hiding in the shadows, embittered perhaps by the failure of 'So Young'.

And it *was* a failure, too! One recalls their then manager, Howard 'Ginger' Jones, rushing through Piccadilly train station, doling out white labels to, it seemed, anyone remotely connected with the music business, utterly convinced that he was holding some kind of latter-day 'Anarchy In The UK'. Quite rightly, of course, as he was the manager. But, back in Stockport, at the legendary Strawberry Studios, a gulf was widening between the band and idiosyncratic producer Martin Hannett. It had been the band's first time in a serious studio, so they placed themselves at the mercy of this unpredictable hedonist (who had, in truth, stumbled off the cutting edge half a decade before). Nothing other than this heavily flawed but highly collectable single would emerge from the sessions.

Two years rolled by and the Stone Roses seemed to be doing little more than posing inelegantly, screaming from the sidelines, eternally adrift if not forgotten. The twin thrusts of the new Manchester, the dance-orientated Haçienda and the more traditional International Club – backed up, lest we forget, by the smaller, keener Boardwalk venue – had, at last, provided the platform for the city's village-like atmosphere to slowly expand. In mid-'86, at the Factory-run week-long extravaganza, The Festival of the Tenth Summer – a mass of gigs presenting the best of Manchester past and present, culminating in a climactic finale at the ill-equipped G-Mex Exhibition Hall – passed by with the Stone Roses adding little more than a shadowy sideshow. They were ageing fast. Their chance, it seemed, had passed.

But strange forces were at work and one of them was manager of the International, Gareth Evans: a flamboyant, mouthy entangle of shadowy entrepreneurialism, unpredictability, ego-fuelled positivity, wayward predictions, wild scammy schemes and curious work patterns. He would flit around town in a Range-Rover, ignoring all manner of by-laws, parking here, there and everywhere, forever shadowed by his accountancy assistant, the loyal Matthew Cummings, often carrying the previous night's International takings in a plastic bag. This former co-owner of a south Manchester hairdresser chain was, contrary to popular rumour, far from stupid. He noticed, for instance, a less than subtle change in the International gig-goers: an intriguing switch from the student swell, to a more riotous, predominantly laddish, working-class norm. This was particularly evident during two infamous gigs performed by north Manchester band the Chameleons; another terminally unhip tribe who, unlike the Roses, had managed to craft an enormous following and, for that matter, stunningly large record sales.

Immediately adopting the mantle of Stone Roses manager, Evans feverishly set about dangling his act in front of the faces of Chameleons fans, using his 'underground' influence to pepper the city centre with a noticeably disproportionate number of posters. Whatever else he might have been, Gareth Evans was no slacker. His feverish work on the band's behalf saw him endlessly spinning spiel into a phone. One night, in pursuit of an article in the *Manchester Evening News*, he dragged the entire band around to my flat and pushed them through the door, practically demanding that I should interview them while the lads, I noted, sat open-mouthed and submissive. It was a strange situation, as if they were relieved to heave the promotional hassles onto the willing shoulders of Evans.

For a band who, throughout their career, wasted no opportunity to state how they wouldn't, at any cost, be dictated to by a record label, their submission to Hurricane Evans still seems astonishing. For example, there was the managerial contract, which provided Evans and Cummings with equal shares to the four band members. Hence this managerial duo were effectively granted 33 per cent of all incoming monies. This alarming situation was exacerbated by the addition of a third member to the managerial team: Lyndsey Reade, manager of funk outfit 52nd Street and ex-wife of Factory Records boss Tony Wilson.

A quaint, addictive melodic single, 'Sally Cinnamon', appeared on the unlikely rock label FM/Revolver and, despite failing to stimulate large sales, at least pulled the band closer to the heart of the burgeoning Manchester scene (the song slotting in neatly alongside James, New Order and the Smiths on 'indie night' student discos).

Much that happened during Evans's reign would·be farcical. Although contracted to produce an album with FM/Revolver, it soon became clear that relations with the company were becoming, to say the least, strained. When Revolver re-issued the 'Sally Cinnamon' single, complete with a promo video that the band hadn't agreed to do, the band abruptly dumped the label. Later, three band members burst into Revolver's Wolverhampton office and covered label boss Paul Birch, his girlfriend and all the surrounding equipment with blue paint. It was a publicity stunt, of course, a fact perhaps given away by the phone call that Birch had received that morning from the NME when a female voice asked, 'Have the Stone Roses arrived yet?'

Lyndsey Reade soon settled into Evans's bizarre office, learning not to laugh when her partner would scream into a phone, 'Hang on ... I've got another call waiting,' place his hand over the mouthpiece and wink at Reade (there was only one phone in the office). Five minutes later he would resume his conversation.

A gig at Camden Dingwalls brought Rough Trade boss Geoff Travis into the picture. After seeing just one song, he turned to Reade and said, 'I'll sign them.'

'I thought, God that was easy. Before that I always had to fight and fight to secure any kind of deal, but Travis, who has great 'ears', was utterly convinced. He wanted them and, as far as I was concerned ... that would soon be that.'

Except that it wasn't. Evans instructed Reade to conduct the ongoing negotiations with Travis and things seemed to progress swiftly. 'I want to do the first single with Rough Trade,' stated Evans. Unknown to Reade however and, it seems, to the band themselves, Evans had started talking to the larger Zhomba Records who would eventually secure the band's signatures. Bizarrely, on the very day that The Stone Roses signed to Zhomba, Gareth Evans attended a marketing meeting with Geoff Travis at Rough Trade, who still thought they would be putting out the single.

'I still can't believe what he (Gareth) did,' states Reade today, 'but that was the end, really, for me. I knew something was afoot, that day, so I rang Gareth and asked him and he said, 'Oh, they have signed. 'Incredible. I still don't know what Gareth's game was ... but he never told me about Zhomba. I presume he hadn't told Geoff either.' If you multiply this odd little scenario by say, 50, you may begin to grasp the bizarre plot shadowing the Roses' success that would eventually, and rather sadly, lead to the law courts. And cause the numbing apathy that squeezed all the creative drive from, potentially, one of the finest bands of all time.

But if this portentous sub-plot looked less than healthy, on the surface, everything seemed rosy. I recall meeting with Evans, Brown and Squire, inside the café at Manchester's Cornerhouse arts centre, nibbling broccoli quiche (uncompromisingly *street*, these boys) ... and there they would sit, again silently, again adopting rock-star grace. People, I noted, turned to stare. I doubt that any of them, being bearded chino-d film-buff whimsies, had any idea who the Stone Roses were, but still they stared. These lads really did look famous, with Squire's fringe flopping over puppy-dog features and Brown's cheekbones practically piercing his flesh.

'But Gareth,' I noted, not unreasonably I thought, 'you haven't sold any records yet.'

'I know,' he replied, 'that's what I keep telling these lads ...'

Things were to change almost instantly. Two spine-tingling singles, 'Elephant Stone' and 'Made of Stone' – written about Brown's Kerouacian wanderings – preceded a debut album, *The Stone Roses*, that immediately assumed 'classic' status. 'If the Stone Roses never release another record,' one critic noted, unwittingly making one of the most prescient statements of the era, 'then they will still have achieved greatness.'

The Madchester explosion was, for the Roses and for most Mancunians, a mixed blessing. For a while though, the downside of being punched into the forefront of the international music media, while hardly being blessed with commanding eloquence, didn't seem to matter. The party had begun.

In July 1989 in, of all places, inelegant Blackpool, 6,000 Mancunian floppies sauntered loosely up and down the prom, furnishing themselves with plastic Reni hats, eagerly tanking up for the Roses performance that evening at the town's Empress Ballroom. It was to be, arguably, the most perfect evening of their career, with Ian Brown whirling around with a red and blue yoyo, swiftly purchased from the prom that afternoon and duly transformed into the perfect rave item. It was at Blackpool, I suggest – rather than at more high-profile appearances at North London's Alexandra Palace, or in Paris, or even at the mighty Spike Island bash – that the Stone Roses truly displayed their power … their, alas, unfulfilled potential.

For it became obvious, that night, that the Stone Roses were successfully selling traditional rock angles to the rave generation. And it wasn't, as has so often been reported, a case of cross-over, of some stupid dance/rock frontline. That was all press bullshit, the kids knew. It was the all-encompassing sense of … attitude. Nothing new in that. Think of Miles Davis, turning his back on the audience, treating them with disdain even. Think of John Lydon during the highly inept P.I.L. performance at Leeds Futurama Festival in 1989, not giving a damn that 11,000 kids had waited 12 hours to catch a glimpse of the back of his head ... and P.I.L. couldn't even be bothered to tune their guitars ... but it worked. Think of Mark E. Smith ...

Ian Brown was the man. He could be as obnoxious as he liked. He could and, during the next couple of years, often did, sit at the side of the stage, adrift in glorious aloofness. In November 1989, this attitude would surface, in spectacularly entertaining manner, during the band's live performance in the studio of BBC 2's cosily anarchic the *Late Show*. Hilariously, the band's in-studio volume would blow the Beeb's fuses, literally, leaving Ian Brown to hurl a stream of insults ('Amateurs' being perhaps the most cutting) at a hapless, harassed Hampstead-ish presenter. Great fun, especially as the broadcast appeared while the band were at the height of their penetrative powers, just prior to their sell-out appearance at Alexandra Palace (an event which lies entrapped on film, in rusting cans, somewhere within the corridors of Granada Television).

Unknown to the Roses, or their fans, or the press or, most tellingly, the Stateside record company execs – who, swallowing the type, sensing an uprising of U2-ish proportions and sniffing sell-out stadiums throughout the nineties, began floating disproportionately meaty offers in the vague direction of Gareth Evans – the game was already up. The band who, in print, endlessly, had stated that they would be 'much bigger and more important than the Rolling Stones' had already tipped over the edge. Spiritually, perhaps, they had already passed the baton across to a young fan named Liam Gallagher who dedicated his young life towards the uncompromising pursuit of shameless full-blown rock stardom. He had soaked in a life-changing blast of celebrated attitude from Brown at a Manchester Roses gig.

And who, in March 1990, as the band sauntered casually on-stage in front of 30,000 revellers on an expanse of tufty shingle near Widnes, would have thought that the Stone Roses, this all-powerful mess of style and stance and melody, had already started to peel away from the intended course. They still seemed to be unstoppable and yet . . . and yet, a cancerous apathy had eaten deep into their desire. Sources close to the band had already started to throw curious accusations of 'lazy bastards/pop stars/arrogant sods'. The implosion was in place.

But, like the Roses at the outset, the implosion came slowly . . . very slowly. The dim, grey, drizzly clouds of litigation began to gather: initially with the band's successful attempt to prize themselves from the clutches of Silvertone (Zhomba) and then, ludicrously, came the inevitable and, it seemed, endless legal scrap with the jettisoned Gareth Evans. This sordid and highly visible affair from which, eventually, Evans would emerge triumphant, would forever taint the memory of the Roses. But, after signing to Geffen for a quite extraordinarily bloated advance, the band retreated into the farmhouses of Wales . . . and into impending middle age. The world waited . . . and waited . . . and waited.

And slowly came The Second Coming. No rock artefact had ever emerged so sluggishly from the horizon. Stretching the anticipation of the fans to and beyond the limit. Legend now informs us that it took one year to make but four previous years to drag the band out of bed. And, in retrospect, there is much to admire on The Second Coming. But to satisfy that thirst of fandom, it had to be more than merely admirable. More than merely great. It would have had to have been fuelled by youthful desperation, polished by class and simply brimming with unfettered originality. Could such an album have been made by four lads softened by money, fame, success, apathy, age, disharmony?

Just after I was asked to write this, I flicked a switch and invited Radio One back into the room ... and to my delight the room was, once more, filled with the delicate, beauteous simplicity of 'Waterfall'. Being profoundly Mancunian, I am proud of Oasis. And one day, I mused, perhaps they too will reach *that* level of perfection.

22

Accept Yourself

New Year's Eve, 1995: Chris is walking through
Didsbury when a car pulls up at a bank on the corner. Out strides Bonehead towards the cash machine.
(There's an interesting balance slip: 'You are three
million pounds in credit. Have a nice day.')

'All right, Bonehead. What are you doing round here
– are you out tonight?'

'All right, Chris. Nah, I can't get a baby sitter, can I?!'

'Did you get to see the Roses then?'

The Stone Roses have just performed two ecstatic
nights at the Apollo in town, a live Second Coming
which Chris had waited over five years to witness.

'Too fuckin' right! Blew my fuckin' mind. Squire
blew me away. John Squire, he's just . . .just . . .'

For all the lads in the Rain, adjectival failure was
a common problem when discussing Squire's guitar work.

'Best band this city's ever produced, the Roses,'
remarks Chris, before realizing what he's implying.

Bonehead grins back, without demurral. 'Anyway, we're off to Germany in a bit – just gettin' some readies. You look after yourself, Chris.'

He seemed to mean that last aside sincerely. Chris still found Bonehead a hard guy to dislike. And seeing the gleam in his eye when he spoke of Squire told Chris that Bonehead's fire was not out yet. Maybe he wouldn't be happy spending the rest of his days as a non-writing rhythm guitarist in someone else's project after all. What was it Blur's Graham Coxon had said? 'I couldn't cope with being a guitar player in Oasis. Just standing there like Bonehead, strumming all night. It'd drive me mad.' Nevertheless, the fat wads of the order Bonehead was counting on the way back to his car must've been some consolation . . .

Equally pleasant had been Noel, whom Chris had encountered on Market Street a month before. Noel was with Alan White, whom Chris found himself ignoring perhaps out of some subconscious sympathy for Tony Mac. Hand-shakes and civility all round, polite chit-chat, all nicey-nicey . . . for Chris at the time couldn't really single out Noel for special wrongdoing. After all, he had even less of the Rain's blood on his hands than Tony Mac, with whom Chris was now very pally. Noel mentioned they were playing the Nynex Arena, though Chris reflected later that Noel had not quite been matey enough to offer him a ticket. They wished each other the best for the future and went their separate ways: Noel to his limo, Chris to a Number 50 bus.

The bonhomie he could share with the rest would not, however, have extended to Guigs. Perhaps fortunately, their paths never crossed directly. The one time Guigs came back to the area, around the period of his US-tour breakdown, Chris didn't find out he'd been home until it was too late. It had been a strange tale. Tony French's younger brother delivered papers to the house Guigsy's family still owned. One morning on his round, he found Guigsy's door had been completely kicked in. He told the newsagents, who rang the police. They came round and performed a perfunctory search before leaving. But later, a woman across the road claimed she'd seen someone emerge from the house and drive off in a BMW *after* the police left.

The story spread that this character had been upstairs in Guigsy's bedroom, which the police had failed to search – an ashtray full of dimps and several CD cases which had been emptied were discovered. Witnessing what had happened was said to have been the last straw for Guigsy; nobody Chris knows ever heard of him staying in Burnage or Levenshulme again. Like the Gallaghers, he has made his home in London with a southern wife and has severed every contact with his old lads.

There was, however, one close shave. Walking through Manchester, Chris saw Guigsy sat in a taxi at a set of traffic lights. Before he'd even begun to consider strolling over for a chat, he sensed himself 'going' – 'going into one'. All he felt was rage, a taste of bitterness at the back of the throat. He stopped on the pavement, not allowing his anger to propel himself into trouble. Guigsy had seen him too, making eye contact and making as if to give a feeble wave. The lights changed and the taxi moved away, probably to Guigsy's relief and certainly to Chris's. He could handle the rest, no problem, but Guigsy was best avoided. There'd never be another calm reunion such as they'd shared at the university gig. And battering a rock star could only ever be a one-way trip to legal bill ville.

Chris would have one last face-to-face with his nemesis Liam, an encounter that would teach him something sobering about the effects of fame. The venue would be Maine Road, April 1996. Oasis were coming home, home to play two sell-out concerts at their supposed spiritual home. ('I've probably been here more often than you have,' Chris would mutter later as Liam approached.) The hype had been about Oasis saying 'thank you' to the fans, appreciating the debt they owed to their city, even of them emulating the Spike Island vibe. The gigs would prove that Oasis were as cherished in Manchester as any of the past greats and demonstrate that they were still in communion with their worshippers. One could argue that they achieved the Spike Island vibe, but only to the extent that it was a mixed experience, leaving some more disillusioned than inspired.

Controversy dogged the build-up, as local fans complained that outsiders had bought all the tickets on credit card booking lines. Others remarked on the hefty ticket price which appeared to lack any sense of the 'thank you' Oasis had promised. And, as with any Mancunian event of this scale, the touts were running wild, in turn encouraging enraged punters to abandon the usual English codes of queueing and patience. All over the approaches to the stadium, marauding packs of scallies, Cockneys and United lads wreaked havoc. Afterwards, a near riot took place as the crowds spilled out into the middle of local Muslim *Eid* festivities. Chaos reigned as gangs took advantage of the opportunity for a bit of racial aggro, like an updated version of the old Burnage High battles.

Inside, City and United boys had clashed, the normal footballing tensions heightened by the proximity that weekend of City to relegation and United to the Premiership title. Know-nothing southerners hadn't helped by turning up in City shirts in the belief that it was a trendy affectation. Reds had some happy hunting sorting out the ignorant fakers.

Chris was invited to go by Tony French, who'd secured a few tickets from Guigsy which would give them access to the hospitality bars. Chris couldn't believe how dodgy it was outside as the criminal element roared about; though he was amused to find Bez behind him going through the turnstiles in his usual 'maraca'd' state. Up in the relative safety of the Kippax bars, a Burnage/Levenshulme lads' reunion began to swing: everyone from the old days had turned up and proceeded to weed the place out, taking the piss out of every minor celeb who happened by. When an alarmed staff tried to clear them all out, rather cleverly shouting 'Fire! Fire!', most were too stoned to move even if they'd believed them. The Oasis performance largely went ignored – this was the best party they'd all had in months.

A buzzing Chris was swaying contentedly by one of the lifts when the doors sprang open to reveal Liam, a Stone Roses roadie and a heavily muscled minder. Liam bounded forward expansively, thrust out a hand and shouted 'Chrissy H! How yer doing, man?' Though stoned, Chris could see Liam had been transformed. All right, he was always a mouthy swaggerer but now he seemed so larger-than-life, almost like a cartoonish parody of a big-time rock star, swinging about like a monkey on speed, exaggerating every movement and pronouncement.

Tony French, who was stood next to Chris, turned to the Roses roadie and asked what was happening to the band: the roadie informed him that John Squire would definitely be leaving. Suddenly, Liam became frenzied: like some demented town cryer, he began marching about, arms outstretched, yelling 'The Roses are no more! The Roses are no more!' Chris and his mates were stunned. Liam appeared excited and thrilled by the news, whereas they were all appalled. His triumphalist air carried an obvious subtext: with the Roses now gone, there could be no further challengers to the crown. Blur were beaten, the rest nowhere – Oasis were now, indisputably, the most important band in Britain.

It had been less than eight years since Liam stood transfixed at the International, falling under Ian Brown's spell and recognizing what would be his life's ambition. The King was dead – long live King Liam? The new monarch hurled a full can of lager out of the window down onto the Kippax car park below, with a final regicidal holler. Leaving him to his courtiers, Chris headed for the bar. He never saw Liam again. He'd barely recognized the Liam he once knew that afternoon anyway.

Oasis managed to dominate both the music press and the tabloids for most of 1996 and 1997. A remarkable feat for a band who hadn't released a block of new work since the autumn of '95 and whose tour schedule appeared to be much lighter than some of their peers'. The steady drip-feeding of new stories to hungry hacks spoke of a PR master at work somewhere behind the scenes, devoted to keeping the band never more than a week away from a front-page splash. This has maintained a phenomenal interest in the band and contrasts sharply with the silence from the Stone Roses for most of their five-year sabbatical. You need to feed curiosity with tasty morsels along the way; starve it, and death results.

Even in mid-97, Oasis feel as much like a currently active group as ever, a band who are still sharing your universe on a day-to-day basis. They have simply not allowed any of their fan-base to become bored of waiting and find nourishment elsewhere – even though the advent of 'New Grave' and Beck-inspired US weirdo-pop has provided ample temptation.

What they lose via this process is the mystique which attached itself to Manc bands of the past. Certainly, the Roses', Smiths' and New Order's periods of complete and deliberate invisibility and general unwillingness to be media tarts provided them with an aura which Oasis have discarded. In fact, despite the lack of recorded product, the only risk Oasis have run is of over-exposure: no one bothers to tag 'exclusive' to interviews, stories and pictures of the Gallaghers any more, since there is such a surfeit of material. You could argue that this is healthy for a self-proclaimed 'people's band', even a refreshing change from the hermit-like existences of their predecessors. Whatever, it has certainly meant that, despite the Spice Girls' challenge in terms of tabloid column-inches, there has been no escape from Oasis.

That is exactly how it felt to Chris, watching from the sidelines as the Oasis phenomenon exploded. It wasn't just that they were on every radio station every half-hour, or in every other paper he read – you can ultimately choose to avoid those media. It was their ubiquity in public space, the fact that you cannot enter a pub, club or shop without hearing Liam's plangent tones wafting across the room. Try spending an hour or two in Manchester city centre on a Saturday afternoon without hearing at least two Oasis songs. It can't be done. They have become the Muzak of the nineties, in every elevator, changing room and burger-bar; deemed by corporate Britain to be as safe and acceptable as Tina Turner or Lloyd-Webber.

Understandably, this drove Chris to distraction for some time. He couldn't bear to hear a note of their music, since it instantly brought back memories of what they'd had together and of what he'd lost. Worse than that: everyone in Burnage and plenty of lads about the city knew who Chris was and what his role had been. For once, Chris had something in common with Bod Gallagher, who talked in his book of how aggravating it became to be questioned all the time about the band. How many times could Chris answer the question 'How does it feel to see Oasis becoming so massive?' Without going nuts? That there was no escape from Oasis's music and presence was bad enough; but it appeared there could be no escape from his own past either.

Eventually, he got over it. As he increasingly came to terms with what had happened and the distance in time grew, he found a sense of objectivity. Bitterness was replaced by resignation. His belief in Fate helped, and a general attitude of positivity. And where once music had provided a release from the wretchedness of Man United's football, it now worked the other way: turn off the radio, let the microphone gather dust and settle down to watch the classic Cantona Double team instead. So there'd be no time to dwell on what might have been after the '96 Maine Road gigs – there was a Double celebration parade and weekend piss-up in Old Trafford to attend to.

Indeed, by 1996, he'd become quite sanguine, despite the occasional jolt of hearing his own daughter humming the latest Oasis single. He'd stopped looking at Liam and thinking 'It could've been me'; instead telling friends that he reckoned Liam had a decent voice and was an excellent frontman. With cool objectivity, he realized that even if he'd survived the transition from the Rain to Oasis like Guigsy did, he couldn't have accepted a Noel Gallagher dictatorship anyway. Nor could he have enjoyed the music they chose to play. He thinks their material is okay – with the exception of 'Some Might Say' and 'Roll With It', which he loathes – but it just isn't his bag. The simple realization that he'd have had no truck with a non-democratic, populist, rootless band helped enormously. Now, when Oasis come onto the factory's radio, he no longer feels the urge to leap up and smash the speakers. And instead of railing about Guigs and Bonehead having 'sold out', happy to become sidemen in a band whose ideology would once have been alien to them, he opted for a pragmatic, softer view: with all that money and fame dangled before them, how many could honestly resist? To some extent, he had finally achieved closure, putting it all behind him in readiness to lead a normal life – even if that life would inevitably be partly soundtracked by Oasis.

There he would have let all this lie, had not the latter part of 1996 brought forth a glut of rose-tinted revisions of the Oasis story. Once he'd read the Oasis books by Mather, Hewitt and others, he realized he would still have to take one more step to end this chapter in his life: you are reading the result.

23

Back to the Old House

Shortly after Chris began to think about correcting the distortions of the Oasis myth-books he ran into Mark Shenton, Liam's teenage best mate. He smiled when Chris told him of his plans, since he knew better than most what Chris had experienced: 'Surprised it's taken you so long.' Chris asked him how things were going between him and Liam these days.

'They're not. Haven't seen him since '95, since before Tony got the boot.'

'Why not?'

'Well, it's the old story innit? Liam's sold out, if you ask me. He knows where we live but he doesn't want to know. I phoned his mam once, she was top, dead friendly. I asked if she could pass a message on to Liam, 'cos he'd not been on to me and I didn't know how to reach him. She said she'd sort it. I'm sure she did but Liam never got back to me anyway.'

The lads talked about the old days, realizing what a similar situation they were in. Liam used to stay at Mark's overnight all the time, just as Guigsy used to crash at Chris's. They'd met on their first day at secondary school too. Mark used to accompany Liam when his father insisted on taking him DJ-ing to places like Hough End Hall. He'd watched Liam become cock of his year and would swagger around Burnage Boys' Club with him, getting into one or two major punch-ups along the way – though Liam always avoided serious trouble and never had a charge-sheet. At 16, they'd progressed on to the Levenshulme scene together after a couple of years wagging school and taking every drug going – especially magic mushrooms, which were free of course. If they had a few spare beans, Noel would often be corralled into getting their weed supplies sorted.

But in July '91, as Liam ended up in a band on the route to fame, Mark received a four-year prison sentence. Like Guigsy, Liam had always swum just short of the sharks; Mark had plunged right in. Mark needed their friendship now, and wrote several letters to Liam. He replied to four, usually when there was Oasis news to boast about, but never once came to visit – the friendship never really recovered.

Chris saw Mark's brother Steve too, who'd been Noel's constant mate throughout their formative years. They chuckled over Noel's adolescent confusion, going through punk, rockabilly and mod phases without ever getting any given style right. (Though he did manage to find a genuine modette called Elaine to go out with during his Parka Period.) They talked about the Beatles mystery – how Noel never talked about the Fabs and seemed much more in thrall to the Pistols, Damned and even Adam Ant, before succumbing completely to the Smiths. Steve thought Noel to be basically a good kid, never into nicking radios or burglary as the myth-makers would have you believe. His only real illegality was supplying weed to his brother, since sniffing glue – a favourite early-teen pastime – was not actually an indictable offence. He simply loved his music, never happier than when wagging school with Steve, strumming his guitar all day long.

What he was *not* was 'A Rebel'. He genuinely loved the Pistols, whom he always told Steve were his favourite band, but he was the archetypal sub-urban/after-the-event punk, the kind who admires and lusts after the spirit of revolution from afar but would never engage it himself. (The only punk in Oasis is, of course, Liam.) And did Steve still see Noel? No: for some reason, Noel never kept in touch, despite their years as good mates . . . Sometimes, especially early on, Oasis members would bitch a little about how they were treated when they went back home, about the difficulties of dealing with lads whom they'd left behind. Occasionally, some might give a thought to how much more difficult it is for those very lads back in Burnage who don't have the consolation of limitless riches to compensate for severed friendships.

Oasis are never seen in Burnage any more – except for Bonehead. He bought himself a house in the upmarket area between Trafford and Cheshire after a couple of years in the band and has popped up in his old haunts a few times. His former contemporaries wonder whether he's tried moving away like the others and found it wanting, preferring to return to the familiar and comforting. Certainly, his old lads were surprised when they started receiving calls from Bonehead, saying he was back in the area and that they should get together.

Not long after Bonehead's return, mad rumours started circulating about encounters with Bone, including stories about money and cars being offered to old mates. Most of it was Burnage bullshit but one persistent bit of blarney suggested that Bonehead was not just a rhythm guitar puppet but that he contributed to the musical compositions more than anyone realized. Was this just mates pumping up his role in the face of accusations that he had artistically sold out? Or was this another example of Gallagher credit-hunger – like the minor kerfuffle over 'Columbia' to which Liam and Tony Griffiths had apparently contributed without legal recognition? Paolo Hewitt later firmly told *Record Collector*, in response to rumours about possible Bonehead/Guigsy input, that 'Oasis music is all Noel's work', before rather patronizingly congratulating the sidemen for their inter-fraternal diplomacy. But those who knew Bonehead do still wonder about the extent of his contribution to Oasis – especially Chris, who saw first-hand the importance he attached to his own music.

Chris hears the latest from Guigsy only through

intermediaries. Since the university gig in '94, he's only had one direct contact with Guigs. Concerned that they'd left their relationship in an awkward no-man's land between cordiality and hostility, Chris resolved to find some sort of easy truce. He got a number for Guigs and suggested they go out for a drink sometime, as old mates keeping in touch. 'Yeah, sure,' replied Guigs, 'when we get back from the States, I'll ring you and we'll do it.' Later, Tony French told Chris what Guigs had said to him as soon as he replaced the receiver:

'I'm not going out anywhere with that cunt.'

And on that charming note, matters rested. Or at least they did until early 1996, when the *Daily Mirror* came sniffing around Chris's house, attempting to door-step him for his story. He refused to speak, virtually having to buy the reporter off by giving her some photos of the Rain in concert, which have proved untraceable since the paper dispensed with her services. Other media enquiries met with the same response: Chris didn't want to talk. Whatever had gone on between him and Oasis was for the lads to resolve. As long as they gave him public respect, he saw no need to speak.

His attitude changed completely when the first rash of Oasis books appeared later in 1996. Liam once said of Noel: 'Our kid should be given a degree in feeding people bullshit stories.' To Chris, it seemed that such an epithet could be applied to the whole band. Where he'd expected to find some mention and credit for his own role, he found a void, as if he and the Rain had been airbrushed out of the historical picture. And where he found the odd reference, it would either be wrong, insulting or grotesquely distorted. Writers couldn't even get the name of his band or the titles of their songs right. And they'd fallen completely for the various myths the members had constructed for themselves. Both of which he could live with – what hurt was the attitude displayed by Liam, Bonehead but especially Guigs towards him as a person and former colleague. Chris had never asked for anything and had never embarrassed them publicly – so why the assassination? Tony Mac would tell Chris: 'I can't believe how you've coped with all this bullshit.' One way to cope suggested itself: write your own story and tell the truth.

When Guigs heard Chris was doing a book, he first affected to be unconcerned. A week later, however, he had a water-carrier transmit the blunt message: 'Anything out of order and I'll sue.' Perhaps they'll be the last words Guigs ever says to Chris, since this book is a true and honest account, written without malice but with resignation. As Chris once remarked about his ousting: 'The difference between me and Guigs is this – if Mani himself had asked to join the Rain, I'd have said no, because it would've meant shitting on my mate. I thought things had come too far between us for him to think otherwise, had he faced a similar choice. I always believed in destiny, so I've got to accept it was meant to be.' And then, with a grin, 'Still, I wish I'd given him a good battering just the once whilst I had the chance!'

Definitely? 'Well . . . maybe. Perhaps it *is* better to say don't look back in anger?'

Index